CW00373644

COOKING IN RETIREMENT

Books by Dan Lees

FICTION

The Rainbow Conspiracy
Zodiac
Rape of a Quiet Town
Elizabeth R.I.P.
Our Man in Morton Episcopi
Mayhem in Morton Episcopi

NON FICTION

Beginner's Luck
The Champagne Fitness Book
Offbeat Somerset

COOKING IN RETIREMENT
Dan and Molly Lees

CHRISTOPHER HELM
London

© 1987 Dan and Molly Lees
Line drawings by Lorna Turpin
Photographs by Martyn K. Williams

Christopher Helm (Publishers) Ltd, Imperial House,
21−25 North Street, Bromley, Kent BR1 1SD

British Library Cataloguing in Publication Data

Lees, Dan
    Cooking in retirement.
    1. Cookery   2. Aged—Nutrition
    I. Title   II. Lees, Molly
    641.5′627   TX652

    ISBN 0-7470-2001-9

Typeset by Florencetype Ltd, Kewstoke, Avon
Printed and bound in Great Britain

CONTENTS

List of Colour Plates

Between pages

Foreword

I love to feel I had something to do with this book seeing the light of day, even if it was simply by sowing the seed on my 'Dear Katie' page in the *TV Times*, and saying that I felt there was a definite call for it.

I did not, however, envisage the charming and original way Dan and Molly Lees would tackle the subject of cooking in retirement. I'm captivated by their combination of fun and common sense; and Molly's talent for encouraging house, garage and even barren brick walls to spring into productivity is little short of inspired. They realise full well that even people with time on the hands aren't all that keen to slave over a hot stove for hours, and they turn their pre-kitchen 'gardening' into a most enjoyable pastime.

Their marrow-draped fences and courgette-packed tubs appeal to me enormously as do their rose-petal-flavoured vinegar, burnet and lemon balm leaves. I feel sure that this book will be read as much for pleasure as for its practical content.

Katie Boyle

Introduction

There are many reasons why cooking in retirement can be more rewarding and more fun than cooking before we quit work. And if that sounds unlikely, it is only because the word retirement is one which should have been put out to grass long ago. After all, it is no way to describe the exciting change from the demanding routines of a full-time job to the challenge of a new life style in which, perhaps for the first time, we are in control of the day-to-day rhythms of our existence.

Maybe retirement, with its undertones of abandonment and resignation, was adequate to describe the situation of many older people in the past, whose lives were considered to be almost over once they gave up their job and went home with their ominously symbolic presentation clock. It is certainly no way to describe what ought to be the beginning of a whole new adventure in living; but unfortunately it's the only word we have, so we're stuck with it.

Cooking in Retirement it is then. But the inadequacy of the word, as well as its catch-all nature, does mean that we are going to have to make clear that to us retirement entails simply no longer having a routine job and in no way argues resignation from the rest of the human race. Nowadays retired people can be forty-five-year-olds with bomb proof pensions, former company chairmen doing very nicely thank you or nonegenarians eking out a relatively tough existence on modest pensions and allowances. However, despite the tremendous range of ages and incomes there are a number of factors common to all retired people.

For one thing, they all have to eat − a fact which alone makes cooking in retirement vitally important. For those of us over forty, good nutritious food is more essential than at any time since we were children; it can not only add to the quality of life but may well extend it.

Fortunately, whether retirement means giving up work completely or changing to a less routine occupation, there are tremendous advantages in being retired, not the least being that retired people usually have more time at their disposal than working folk and, when it comes to cooking, time really is money. As a retired person, for instance, you have time to plan your meals, along with the rest of your activities, to suit yourself and, while there is no need to lay down a hard and fast schedule in advance, a little forethought can help ensure that meals are nutritious, interesting and, if need be, economical.

There's usually time, too, to grow some foodstuffs, if only mustard and cress or a few lettuce and cherry tomatoes in a window box. Or, if you have a garden, even if it is only a small back yard, you can grow a surprising amount of fruit and vegetables − all well worth having for the sake of freshness and flavour, as well as for the obvious cash saving.

Having time to shop is another thing that can save money − or at least make sure that you get the very best value for the money you spend; and with a few minutes to spare, you may even enjoy practising the gentle art of haggling.

1

There's also time to gather some of the few things in the world that are still free, like blackberries, elderberries and field mushrooms. No matter how much money you have it's pleasant to know that, for retired people at least, there can be such a thing as a free lunch.

Of course while having time to plan, shop, grow and gather is useful, it is having time to prepare the food that makes all the difference. Although it is sometimes difficult to get used to the idea, once you are retired you don't have to worry too much about the odd meal being a few minutes late — unless of course you have your own reasons for wishing to be punctual. You can take your time, which makes it a lot easier to get dishes exactly as you want them and also enables you to put a little extra effort into the presentation, which is often enough to turn an ordinary meal into something special.

One thing that worries people facing retirement is that they may have difficulty living on less money than was available when they were working. In many cases these fears prove to be groundless, so it is as well to wait and see how things work out, rather than plan to economise on essentials like food.

Retirement brings its own economies and it's unlikely, for example, that you will find yourself having to lunch out, as most working people do. Commuting, too, will no longer be the constant expense that it was and, if you worked in an office, you probably won't have to spend anything like as much money on clothes.

Many people by the time they reach retirement age have already acquired most of the expensive consumer items they need; the mortgage may well be paid up and the car no longer owned by the finance company, while spoiling grandchildren — as opposed to bringing up one's own children — tends to be a pleasant bit of occasional self-indulgence rather than a constant financial drain.

At the same time a number of those payments that make the bank balance look sick every month when your standing orders are paid suddenly stop. You may no longer, for instance, have to find money for National Insurance, pension plans and the like and, in many cases, people actually begin paying you.

Another saving is that you no longer have to spend money on expensive convenience foods, although they are too handy to deprive yourself of them altogether; you can make use of them in emergencies if need be, but usually you should find that having a little time to spare means that you can make dishes that are tastier, more nutritious and cost only a fraction of ready-prepared food.

Of course, economy may not be a prime consideration but it's usually pleasing to save money, especially when it can be done without any lowering of standards. That's why we've devoted quite a lot of attention to the question of getting value for money, saving cash where possible and have added some recipes for hard times — just in case.

I left my last full-time job in 1965, since when there have been times when we have been relatively rich and others when we have been relatively poor. On the whole I suppose we would have to agree with the man who said 'Rich is better' but we had a lot of good times when we were broke and always managed to eat well.

To be fair it is a lot easier to enjoy yourself when you're broke if you are reasonably confident that the condition is not permanent. Even so, we did go through some hard times when we were living abroad and had to learn how to cope, especially when it came to putting food on the table.

One thing we discovered was that if a trouble shared is a trouble halved, a meal shared can be a meal doubled and that by pooling resources with friends whose incomes were as small and unreliable as our own, we could make everything spin out that much further and have fun at the same time.

Certainly we managed to stay very healthy, due partly no doubt to the fact that even if some of our meals were sparse they were usually unhurried, which is another great advantage retirement can bring. Obviously as one gets older sensible eating assumes even greater importance than before and, while we are by no means faddists, there is a lot to be said for a balanced diet with plenty of fresh fruit and vegetables, so we have included some thoughts on nutrition and a few recipes which will enable you to lose weight if you need to do so.

People living on their own, whether retired or not, often find it difficult to become enthusiastic about cooking. It's so easy to get by for a while on toast and TV dinners that eventually low quality food, with all its attendant miseries, becomes a way of life. One way to combat this is to make easily prepared food more exciting; it really is almost as easy — and much more fun — to make a tasty snack as it is to open a can. And if you do reach for the can opener every now and again you can turn, say, a run of the mill soup into something much more interesting by throwing in a few extra ingredients.

People living alone can find a new interest in preparing tasty meals for themselves and to help them we've included lots of ideas on cooking for one person, although most of the recipes — unless otherwise indicated — are for two people.

Social life shouldn't end with retirement; in fact, retired people may well find that now they have more time to stop and chat they will have the chance to make more friends than when they were working. Of course they may well miss the ready-made links and the shop talk of the work place, but it's not impossible to meet people who have retired from the same line of work as one's self, especially if you are able to invite them to share a meal.

This will probably lead to a reciprocal invitation from people who, with luck, are also interested in good food, so to help with this we've included a section about entertaining on a budget.

Of course entertaining is as important for couples as it is for retired people living on their own but at least the singles do have one advantage in that they are able to decide when they want to have company.

Retired couples, on the other hand, often find that no matter how close they may be, and how good the relationship, being together for most of every day as opposed to weekends and a few hours in the evenings entails a certain amount of adjustment.

As we very quickly discovered when I gave up working from an office and began working at home, life as a full-time partnership is very different from life as a couple whose time together is dictated by the need for long hours and frequent business trips. It's easy for the greatest of lovers and the best of friends to get on each other's nerves if they are not used to being together all the time but, with luck, it soon becomes apparent that there are positive advantages to facing life as a full-time team.

Cooking in retirement can help couples develop this sort of team spirit, provided both parties are prepared to share the load of cooking — and the fun.

Shared achievements — and even the odd shared disaster — in the kitchen mean that *Cooking in Retirement* can make retirement as enjoyable and exciting as it should be.

With luck — if the way to a man's or woman's heart really is through the stomach — it could even turn your retirement into an extended second honeymoon. While we can't promise that, we can at least hope that you have as much fun trying out the dishes as we had in working them out in the first place.

Acknowledgements

We would like to thank the following people for their help in the preparation of this book: Lynn Bresler, Melanie Crook, Ann Doolan, Tony Ferrand editor of Golden Age, Jenny Harris, Jo Hemmings, Tom and Laura Howard, Dr A.B. Lavelle, Nell Lines, Jane Roberts, Barbara Rees Regional Director Age Concern, George and Nini Robinson, Ted and Dorothy Rogerson, John Sansom, Richard Wigmore, Martyn Williams.

1

Shopping in Retirement

The ideal situation for a cook — retired or otherwise — would be a fully equipped, professionally staffed kitchen with one door opening onto a kitchen garden and the other leading to a permanently open supermarket. That way all you would have to do would be to decide on a menu — always one of the fun parts of cooking — and then send one of the staff to pick fruit and vegetables while another went off to do the shopping.

The ingredients for every dish would be immediately available and rushed back to your kitchen within minutes, while other staff prepared to do the rough work as you, in your capacity as master chef, made ready to orchestrate their efforts, tasting at every stage and accepting or rejecting their offerings with a casual gesture as the meal took shape.

All you would need then — apart from your own merchant bank — would be enough expertise to compose your culinary masterpiece and, as a visit to any good restaurant will show, this method works. Superb ingredients plus first class equipment, plus good kitchen skills and expertise, with the addition of a pinch of genius, really do make for wonderful meals.

Unfortunately most of us have to do the best we can with limited funds, fairly ordinary kitchens and one person's help if we are lucky. Fortunately, however, retirement enables us to make up for many of the handicaps that plague working folk who like to cook — mainly because retired people have more time at their disposal and, as I've pointed out, when it comes to cooking, time genuinely is money.

Retirement gives you time to think about things like store cupboards which means that while you may not live above a hypermarket your cupboard will never be bare. It can even give you time to think about the cupboards themselves, which ideally should have narrow shelves rather than deep ones and should be placed at a height you find convenient.

In one kitchen we had, we made a useful fitted cupboard on a difficult short wall between two doors. The shelves were only six inches deep and fitted up to the frame of the kitchen door. The whole fitment, which took just one row of bottles, jars or cans, measured 7 inches deep by 54 inches wide and 54 inches high and held an incredible amount.

Of course you may not be planning a new kitchen for some time, if ever, but, if you are, shallow cupboards are the ones to have and, if you are not, it is worthwhile planning so that the things you need all the time are in sight and within easy reach. You can do this either by filling the rear of a deep cupboard with a line

5

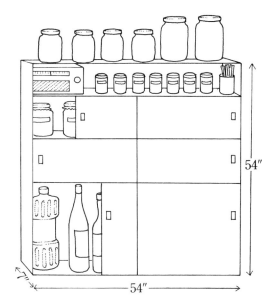

of tall containers, clearly labelled near the top, or by using the space at the rear for your emergency stores.

Common sense of course but, like many of the other things in this book, this is something we learned the hard way − in this case by knocking over bottles, jars and cartons while searching for some small pot which had somehow worked its way to the rear of a cupboard the size of Grand Central Station. We went on doing this for years, sending our blood pressure zooming up like the indicator on a 'test your strength' machine until we worked out that it might be better to put things where we could see them and make it impossible to lose them; we did this by fixing a one inch high batten across the base of the cupboard, about half way back, low enough so that it didn't impede our view of the things behind but high enough to stop small things working towards the back. Simple − but there may well be people who can learn from our mistakes.

For example, one mistake we made when we moved from the centre of a big city to a small hill farm, miles from anywhere, was to imagine that we could still nip out to the shops. For one thing the nearest shops were four miles away at the bottom of a hill like a ski-slope and for another we were frequently snowed in during the winter for weeks at a time which made shopping difficult. We soon learned that a small emergency larder made sense and, while the extent of your stores will be governed both by storage space at your disposal and the amount you

are able to spend, there's a good case, we discovered, for investing in an emergency larder when you have a little money to spare.

Suggested Emergency Stores List

3 lbs self-raising flour
1 lb rice
1 lb pasta
bottle cooking oil
dried milk
1 packet crackers
1 packet dried onion
carton fruit juice

tea/coffee
2 lbs sugar
1 tin each of soup, meat, fish, fruit
1 jar jam/marmalade/honey
Marmite/Bovril
stock cubes or powder
bottle of water (spring water)
candle with holder and matches
    wrapped in plastic

All these emergency stores will fit into a cardboard box at the back of a deep cupboard and would provide the main ingredients of several meals. If you are used to camping stoves, you might add a small one to cope with power cuts. You should also keep a torch on a convenient hook in the kitchen so you can find your emergency stores if the lights go out!

Some of our favourite recipes came out of our emergency stores, including The Easiest Bread in the World. Molly found it under that heading in her mother's notebook when we ran out of bread one Bank Holiday. 'This will never work,' she said. 'Mother must have missed something out.' But she tried it just the same and in less than an hour we were eating an excellent loaf, only slightly heavier than ordinary yeast bread. We have made it many times since then and found it is equally good with wholemeal flour if you add a teaspoon of baking powder.

 # The Easiest Bread in the World

Preparation time: 10 minutes
Cooking time: 35 minutes

Imperial (Metric)

1 lb (450 g) self-raising flour
1 heaped teaspoon salt
½ pint plus 2 tablespoons (305 g) water

American

4 cups self-rising flour
1 heaped teaspoon salt
1½ cups water

1. Mix all the ingredients in a bowl until they form a ball.
2. Turn out onto a floured bowl and knead lightly.
3. Shape into a round and place on a well greased baking sheet or press into a greased loaf tin (pan).
4. Bake for 35 minutes on the middle shelf of a pre-heated oven (425°F/220°C/Gas Mark 7).

Variation You can also shape it into small breakfast rolls which take 15 to 20 minutes cooking time. We usually make two loaves at a time, adding 2 oz (50 g)

(½ cup raisins) to the second to make Raisin Tea Bread.

The Traditional Scottish Oatcakes recipe came from the same notebook and is useful for the times when you run out of biscuits for cheese. It is one of those good simple and economical recipes you find in most countries, where the cheapest native ingredients are made into excellent food.

 # Traditional Scottish Oatcakes

Preparation time: 15 minutes
Cooking time: 30 minutes

Imperial (Metric)

6 oz (175 g) fine oatmeal
1 oz (25 g) wholemeal flour
pinch salt
enough water to make a stiff dough

American

1½ cups fine oatmeal
1 heaped tablespoon wholemeal flour
pinch salt
enough water to make a stiff dough

1. Whizz breakfast oats in a blender if you have no fine oatmeal.
2. Mix ingredients with water to make a stiff dough.
3. Roll out on a floured board until very thin, sprinkling with flour if it sticks, and cut into rounds with a 2½ inch (6 cm) cutter.
4. Bake for 30 minutes on the top shelf of a pre-heated oven (stove) at (350°F/180°C/Gas Mark 4) for 30 minutes until very slightly coloured.

These should be eaten within two or three days but you can keep oatcakes much longer in a tin or screw top jar if you add 2 heaped tablespoons (50 g) of butter or bacon fat to the dry ingredients before stage 2.

Of course, although there may be times when you can't get to the shops, the emergencies which may occur from time to time are not always a question of logistics. There may be other times when you don't feel too great, when funds are low or when life seems just too much trouble. These are life's genuine emergency emergencies and this is where the space behind the barrier or behind the big containers in your store cupboard can come in handy − because in addition to your emergency items you could include a box of chocolates, a tin of sweets (candies), a couple of miniatures of your favourite liqueur or some other delicacy.

In this way, at the very time you need to raid your emergency larder − which almost by definition will not be a laugh a minute time − you'll discover a little treat that, with luck, you had forgotten all about.

Basic Stores

Basic stores are not the same thing as emergency stores but much the same factors govern some of your choices, like the size of your storage space, the size of your bank balance and whether you have a big refrigerator and freezer.

One important point − don't stock up on things you don't like. It's no use cluttering up your cupboards with tins of beans and pilchards if you can't stand them. They are not a bargain if you never eat them.

With heavy items like potatoes, it is a good idea to buy in 28 lb or even 56 lb sacks. They are a marvellous stand-by vegetable, they store well and if you try to shop for them weekly you'll find your shopping bag full before you start on anything else.

The storage times on the following list of basic items refer to *unopened* packets, cans or jars.

Up to six months:	flour (white), dried yeast, baking powder, bicarbonate of soda, cream of tartar, breakfast cereals, dried fruits.
Up to a year:	tea, instant and ground coffee (sealed), dehydrated goods, custard powder, dried milk, most herbs and spices, canned fruit, canned fish in tomato sauce, brown sugar, jams.
Up to two years:	canned vegetables, vinegars, cooking oil, packet jellies (jello), ketchup (catsup).
Long life:	cornflour (cornstarch), pasta, rice, white sugar, honey, marmalade, treacle (molasses), syrup, canned fish in oil, canned meat (small tins only), pepper, salt, mustard powder, yeast and beef extracts, cocoa.

Of course you'll have your own ideas on what you want to store but the above suggestions could help when you are stocking your cupboards.

Don't forget to check your Emergency Stores every six months, removing and using short life items and replacing them with fresh purchases.

Shopping

Shopping for food, like shopping for anything else, can be fun; but unless your shopping expeditions are planned, they can endanger your pocket and your health.

The answer, much as it goes against the grain, is to make a shopping list before you set out − and stick to it. Don't forget that the store owners are doing their best, by making everything look very attractive, to lure you into the impulse buys which will pay for their foreign holidays.

Harden your hearts; but on the other hand don't make shopping into a totally regimented occupation. Allow for fun purchases by including an amount, however small, for Item X on your list. That way, if you spot a bargain or something you particularly fancy that is not on your list you can snap it up, provided it comes within the amount you have put aside. If you see nothing that tempts you, you can either bask in the feeling of virtue and put the money back into the housekeeping or allow twice the amount for Item X next time you go shopping.

Making a list takes much of the stress out of shopping as you know exactly what you are looking for and roughly how much you are going to spend. If you cross off each item as you buy it you won't forget something vitally important and have to go back for it which, if you are a day dreamer like me, is a boon.

Shopping in retirement is different from shopping when you have to go to work, because instead of being rushed you should have time to shop effectively. No more dashing into a store, trying to make up your mind what you are going to have for dinner, because whether it's a couple of items or a truckload you will know exactly what you want.

Compiling a shopping list sounds easy but it can be tricky unless you know what is in your store cupboard, and which items are running low and need replacing. This is where a kitchen reminder list comes in handy. It has no need to be elaborate — one of those re-usable plastic notice boards would do nicely.

The lists we feel are absolutely essential are:

Emergency Stores List
Kitchen Reminder List
Shopping List (for each trip)
Freezer List

If you have a freezer you might like to keep a list of contents which you can tick off as you use them and add to whenever you buy more. After experimenting with several ideas we have devised a very easy to manage freezer list on a sheet of stiff card which can hang up close to the freezer.

Vegetables	
Peas	̶1̶ ̶1̶ ̶1̶ 1 1 1 1 1
Green Beans	̶1̶ ̶1̶ ̶1̶ ̶1̶ ̶1̶ 1 1 1 1
Corn	1 1 1 1
Sprouts	1 1 1 1 1

Continue through chips (french fries), onion rings, etc. and then with headings of Meat, Fish, Fruit, Pastries, Home Baked Pies, Complete Meals, etc.

Each time you use an item cross it off, each time you buy an item add another 1.

We have also found that if we buy in bulk it's a good idea to divide items like vegetables into 1 lb or ½ lb packs before putting them away.

Of course if you are one of those people who enjoy making lists you could also note down a lot of information which will be a big help with housekeeping, shopping and budgeting. In fact, now that you have more time for such things, you might even like to keep a Shopping Book with lists of stores and entries something like this:

Date	Shop	Purchase	Price	Verdict
1 May	Browns	Bananas	50p	good
1 May	Browns	Mushrooms	25p	not brilliant

This provides a useful guide to your consumption and expenditure, the reliability of individual shops, comparative prices and your ability to get value for money. Not only that but, used in conjunction with a pocket calculator, it might even result in your being taken for some sort of official and given the VIP treatment.

In effect, a shopping book of this sort amounts to organising your own Shopping Intelligence Service, although you should get VIP treatment anyway because, as a customer, you are a Very Important Person. And, what's more, now that you have retired you are in a position to be choosy.

Habits are hard to break and if you've spent your life up to now dashing around like an anxious White Rabbit the fact that you now have time to spare takes some getting used to.

There is no need now, for instance, to dash to your nearest shop which could well be the most expensive. Try several and use your shopping book to identify the pick of the bunch. You could mark the items which have been particularly good value with a red star and check up at the end of the month to see which store has most red stars. Then compare the little corner shop with the supermarket chain. You could, for example, find that the individual shopkeeper will be prepared to sell smaller amounts of things like cheese or ready cooked meats than the supermarkets, although many of these have now realised that customers may want to buy just one apple or one tomato.

You might also spend a little time in the supermarket looking for the 'loss leader' – the item which is usually on sale at a very low price to tempt people into the store. You could make it your Item X, but only if it is something you either need or want.

Try looking at the smaller and slightly less well appointed supermarkets. Remember that someone has to pay the colossal overheads of the giant chains and fork out for all that glass and chrome and, even though they may benefit from the economies of scale, you can bet that some of the cost is added to the price of cornflakes.

As the old army saying goes, 'Time spent in reconnaissance is time well spent' and, as you now have the time, it's well worth spying out the land before a major shopping expedition. You have no need to buy on these recce trips but if you do – provided you limit yourself to what you can comfortably carry or pull in a trolley – the only restricting factor is how far you care to walk.

If you are walking, little and often is the thing. A shopping list is invaluable for this but do stick to it. Both Molly and I have come back from the shops looking like orang-utans with our arms half pulled out of their sockets after setting out to fetch 'a couple of things' – and it not only hurts like hell but can do permanent damage.

Of course everyone's shopping needs vary, as do their facilities; you may be well off or not so well off, drive a car or not, have a huge larder or none at all and possess both a refrigerator and deep freeze or neither.

However, there are a few basic tips to bear in mind, namely:

– Try to do one big shop regularly, say once a month for non-perishable items or freezer goods. For one thing it gets all the rather boring stuff out of the way in one go and for another it's often cheaper to buy loo rolls, washing powder and so on in quantity.

– If you have a car make use of it for this major shop and save petrol by using your shopping list to plan the trip in advance.

– If you are using more than one store, list the items on your shopping list under each store and list the stores in order. This sounds obvious but it's easy to miss out a vital item and realise that you walked or drove past the shop that sells it half an hour before.

– If you don't have a car or a bus going past the door, but do have good friends or members of your family living close enough to drive you to the shops, they will be much happier to do so if you know exactly where you want to go and what you want to buy. Or they may be willing to bring back a few heavy things for you. But remember, as unfortunate working types, they may not have all that much time to spare.

– With no mobile and generous friends or relations things can be a bit tougher, but you might consider doing a deal with your local taxi-driver or car-hire firm. Unless large distances are involved, a taxi once a month – especially for a well planned shopping trip on which no time is wasted – could be the answer.

– No car, nobody willing to provide transport and no money for a taxi? Try looking for a grocer who delivers – they are rare but they do exist – check his prices to make sure they are not too much higher than everyone else's and calculate how much you are going to add on if you buy all your basics from him once a month. Then try to do a deal, offering to do just that, provided he'll deliver for free. He may say no but it's worth a try.

— Another way is to find a strong youngster anxious to earn a little pocket money — although television and inflation have turned most kids of the right age and size into mercenary monsters.

— If you live in a remote village a few like-minded friends might look into the feasibility of hiring a mini-bus for a couple of hours once a month or you might find a car-owning pensioner who will be happy to let you pay for the petrol in return for transport.

Whatever you do, try your utmost not to carry or push too much because it not only takes all the pleasure out of shopping but can lead to back trouble into the bargain. Better by far, if you simply can't get hold of transport or help, to make shopping part of your exercise and walk to the shops a few times a week for a small number of things at a time.

If you are ill and unable to get out to the shops, it is worth while talking to the Social Services Department which will either sort something out themselves or put you in touch with an appropriate voluntary group.

Of course it's usually best if you can manage on your own but it is good to know that there is help available should you need it.

When you are cooking in retirement as opposed to merely making food, you could well wish to show off your skills by inviting people to share a snack or a meal — in fact one of the delightful things about not having to go to work is that it's a lot easier to have friends in for a visit, even if it is only to have a cup of tea or coffee and a home-made biscuit.

We'll be looking at the whole subject of entertaining in retirement later on, but in connection with shopping, it's useful to remember that just one friend who is also retired can double your shopping intelligence capability and make shopping a lot more fun.

Shopping intelligence, as well as keeping you informed about the best shops and the best buys, should also make you aware of which shops are prepared to bargain and if you have the nerve to try it, it can really save you money.

I've never found it very easy to ask for a discount but I have been trying harder recently and have been pleasantly surprised at the reductions I've been able to obtain simply by asking for them. Molly's father was an absolute master of the art. He held that the magic phrase was '. . . and for cash?' and claimed that he never paid the full asking price for anything.

Bargaining for food is a question of picking one's time. Greengrocers and markets, for example, will often sell ripe fruit, mushrooms and salad stuff very cheaply on a Saturday evening if they are closed the following day.

A few years ago we managed to buy Brie very cheaply because the person selling it didn't like runny cheese and was convinced that the delicious rounds of the stuff were going off!

Most supermarkets have a 'bargain basement' counter where you can find stuff that is near its 'sell by' date marked down considerably, together with fruit, packets and cans that have been in the wars. The cans are a good buy if just the label is torn but it pays to be wary if the can itself is damaged. Incidentally, you have no need to feel self-conscious about buying from these bargain shelves because you'll be in good company with not only loads of students and young couples but plenty of obviously wealthy customers, demonstrating how they got to be wealthy in the first place.

I for one always look to see what is on offer and my recent bargains, for example, include a perfect pineapple at half price — incredibly sweet by comparison with the full price ones which were so hard as to be inedible — and a melon at less than half price which was utterly splendid.

It probably won't be necessary to go as far as the Scottish kid I heard of who, on being told by the grocer that he had no broken biscuits, accidentally on purpose dropped a packet and replied, 'Well — you have now!', but it is amazing what you can do when times get hard, as we have discovered once or twice ourselves. Of course, when times are really hard it isn't a question of picking up luxury items cheaply but of making the best possible use of the cheaper foodstuffs.

Sadly, in most Western countries, it's much more difficult nowadays to economise on food than it once was because the things that used to be regarded as the food of the poor — and were priced accordingly — are now relatively expensive. Once, for example, things like flour, rice, sugar and milk cost very little which meant that good managers could feed their families nourishing basic food for something and nothing. Now, however, even food like oats and herrings which kept a lot of Scottish and Jewish families fed during hard times, while still economical, are hardly to be picked up for a few pence.

In France, when we were trying to make ends meet between cheques, we used to buy bread baked the day before — French bread goes hard very quickly — for just a few centimes. Slices dipped in milk and fried made a main course with just one tomato or mushroom and, with the addition of a scraping of marmalade, a pudding as well. We'll be talking about economical recipes in another chapter and the criterion will be that they have to be good enough to eat on those occasions when you are not actively economising.

There are some marvellous meals to be made using the cheaper cuts of meat and inexpensive fish and you'll see what we mean about good enough to eat on any occasion when you try recipes like Nini's Surprise Fish Pie (see p. 173) which was first served to us at a dinner party.

You could also experiment with those inexpensive but rather boring little steaks of frozen cod or haddock when you are tired of serving them with parsley sauce.

Why not try:

 Fish Goujons

Preparation time: 10 minutes
Cooking time: 15 minutes

Imperial (Metric)	American
2 small frozen boneless steaks of white fish	*2 small frozen boneless steaks of white fish*
1 egg, beaten	*1 egg, beaten*
4 oz (110 g) breadcrumbs	*1 cup of breadcrumbs*
1 lemon	*1 lemon*
French mustard	*French mustard*

1. Cut the fish steaks across lengthwise while still frozen and then slice into small sticks — you should get about 24 from each steak.
2. Dip in beaten egg and roll in breadcrumbs.
3. Deep fry about 12 at a time for 3 or 4 minutes until golden brown. Keep hot until all the goujons are cooked.
4. Serve with mustard and lemon wedges.

This quantity makes a first course for four people or a main course for two with the addition of a green vegetable.

You could also try:

 # Baked Fish with Fennel

Preparation time: 20 minutes
Cooking time: 20 minutes

Imperial (Metric)

2 small frozen boneless steaks of white
*   fish*
2 tablespoons chopped parsley
1 teaspoon ground fennel
2 medium mushrooms
1 lemon
2 tablespoons cream
2 flat teaspoons butter

American

2 small frozen boneless steaks of white
*   fish*
2 tablespoons chopped parsley
1 teaspoon ground fennel
2 medium mushrooms
1 lemon
2 tablespoons cream
2 flat teaspoons butter

1. Cut out two squares of tin foil (12 in x 12 in) and put a fish steak in the centre of each.
2. Thinly slice a lemon and the mushroom and divide between the fish. Sprinkle on the fennel.
3. Cover each fish with a tablespoon of cream, then the chopped parsley and butter.
4. Bring up the sides of the tin foil and twist together to keep in the liquid.
5. Put in the oven — top shelf — for 20 minutes at (400°F/200°C/Gas Mark 6).
6. When cooked, drain off the liquid and whizz in the blender. Serve separately as a sauce. This goes well with new potatoes and broccoli.

A fish and vegetable terrine is more trouble but looks stunning on the table and is a good first course for a dinner party. If you are serving it just for two people it is equally good cold next day with salad.

 # Layered Fish Terrine

Preparation time: 40 minutes
Cooking time: 90 minutes

Imperial (Metric)

1 egg, beaten
½ lb (225g) carrots (cooked weight),
*   puréed*
½ lb (225g) spinach (cooked weight),
*   puréed*
2 small boneless fish steaks, poached
*   and flaked*
butter
salt and white pepper to taste

American

1 egg, beaten
8 ounces cooked and puréed carrots
8 ounces cooked and puréed spinach
2 small boneless fish steaks, poached
*   and flaked*
butter
salt and white pepper to taste

Sauce

5 oz (150g) plain thick yoghurt
grated peel and juice of 1 lemon
1 tablespoon chopped parsley
salt and black pepper to taste

Sauce

1 cup thick yoghurt
grated peel and juice of 1 lemon
1 tablespoon chopped parsley
salt and black pepper to taste

1. Place puréed carrots, spinach and fish in separate bowls.
2. Beat up the egg in a tablespoon of water and divide between the three bowls.
3. Butter a 1 lb loaf tin (pan) and press the carrot purée evenly in the base. Make sure it is as flat and even as possible. (An empty loaf tin, the same size, will press it down flat.)
4. Next put in the puréed spinach, then the fish.
5. Cover the top of the tin with foil and place in a shallow roasting tin containing water. Bake for 90 minutes at (375°F/190°C/Gas Mark 5). Leave to cool a little before turning out onto a serving dish.
6. The sauce is made by simply beating up the ingredients to a thick cream.

As a main course the terrine is excellent served with scalloped potatoes — thin slices of potato cooked with a little butter in a shallow dish in the bottom of the oven — and the sauce goes well with both.

Of course the fish steaks are also very appetising dipped in batter and deep fried. The secret of a crisp batter is to use just flour and water — 4 oz (110g) (1 cup) of flour in a deep basin and a dribble of water. Turn the tap (faucet) so that it is just dripping and beat the flour mixture until it is thick and creamy. Add a pinch of salt and your batter is ready to use. Cheap and simple and better than all the batters containing milk and eggs.

When you are shopping for meat, as well as looking at the less expensive cuts, it's often possible to find top quality meat which has been relegated to the cheaper counter because it isn't the right size or weight to match the display of expensive cuts.

You can also find bacon off-cuts sold at half price in 1 lb or 2 lb packs. These are particularly useful: sort out the slices that will grill or fry for breakfast, put pieces for flans, quiche Lorraine, ham and mushroom pie, etc. in small packs in the freezer and make a good ham and green pea broth from the remaining fatty bits.

If you are buying wine, which we tend to regard as a necessity, you can do very well indeed if you look around. Try to find out which wine areas have over-produced in the previous four or so years; the wines won't be anything like as cheap as they really should be, but at least they will be more reasonable than wines from areas where the production has been low. Look too for wines from an area next to a famous wine growing region — you could pick up exactly the same product with a less august label for a lot less money.

The main thing of course is that whatever your income, provided you have enough to live on, you do have the time, now that you are retired, to enjoy your shopping. There's no rush and even if you do forget something — in spite of thoroughly prepared lists and splendid memoranda — there will always be time to pick it up tomorrow, or even the next day.

After all, you are retired and if you can afford anything you can afford to take it easy.

2

Equipment
~A Retirement Rethink

Unlike students, newly weds and most other people who find themselves doing a fair amount of cooking for the first time, retired people usually have a reasonably equipped kitchen and, whether our own culinary domain is large or small, we are used to it.

That of course is the problem. We've soldiered along very nicely up to now, so why bother to change things?

Well, for one thing, it's really amazing what most of us can collect in half a lifetime in the way of pots, pans, kettles and useless gadgets, not to mention the jam jars full of dry ballpoint pens and stubs of pencil.

In our case, not only does Molly have an almost religious objection to throwing anything away but both my mother and hers were similarly attached to domestic objects, which meant that we inherited a large number of artefacts which belonged by rights in some museum of anthropology, including pans and kettles which ought to have gone to make Spitfires in World War II.

Of course we went right on using them, hardly noticing that they were getting dented, chipped and battered to the point where many of them were almost impossible to clean, which made washing up really hard work.

If you too have this sort of collection your first step towards making cooking in retirement a pleasure might well be to decide what kitchen equipment you can throw away.

You can tell if you have a bad case of utensilitis simply by opening a rarely used pan cupboard. If a metallic cascade of battered and ever so slightly rusty saucepans and baking tins clatters to the floor then you should consider immediate action.

Fortunately, unlike starting from scratch, paring down your kitchen equipment costs nothing but time and if you can find a friendly second hand dealer you may even make a little money out of your kitchen antiques.

If financial considerations mean that you have to make do with what you have got, then at least get rid of the very big, heavy and cumbersome items and, if you are too attached to them to throw them out, use them as plant holders or give them to the younger members of your family who could well be glad of them.

For one thing, now that you have retired it's unlikely that you will be required to cook for large numbers on a day-to-day basis. And, for another, the damned things are virtually guaranteed to turn your wrist and scald you, as well as wasting a lot of good grub.

If you are the sort of retired person who works out three times a week at a

Fitness Centre, runs a half marathon before breakfast or regularly plays eighteen holes of golf, this is where you might decide that you don't need to make these changes; after all, if you can exercise with 16 lb dumbbells or whatever you're not going to have much trouble with a saucepan.

The point is that we are aiming to be still cooking when we are a hundred, by which time even I am prepared to admit that I may not be as strong as I was at thirty or even sixty. That being the case, it makes sense to get into good habits which will stand us in good stead later on and to design and equip kitchens which will still be suitable for our needs in a few decades time.

So, let's get rid of all the very heavy items as well as the dented and pitted ones – they can always be used in the garden for flowers and the really big ones can even be used for growing herbs and salads.

At the same time as you are getting rid of the scrap iron you could also throw out any utensils with loose handles. Try using a screwdriver to tighten them, by all means, but if they come loose again be ruthless and get rid of them because even if you are used to the way they wobble around someone else may not be.

Finally you should get rid of all those items which have been 'bound to come in handy' for the last ten years or so, together with all the miracle gadgets that somehow failed to live up to their glowing promise.

In the end it is all a matter of individual circumstances and personal choice but most of us, especially if we are thinking in terms of cooking for ourselves at a hundred, will be able to streamline our kitchens by disposing of things that are too heavy, too old, broken or useless – inanimate things, of course!

Having streamlined your kitchen in this way it's worthwhile looking at what's left and what you need to acquire; perhaps the easiest way is to make a list of what is essential and what would be nice to have if you found yourself with a winning lottery ticket.

We are assuming that you have a cooker but if you are thinking of a replacement, do bear in mind that as you get a bit older you may well find it easier not to have to bend down to a low oven and a high level fitted one is probably a good idea.

We have also assumed that most people who are cooking in retirement will have a refrigerator, a virtually essential piece of kitchen equipment, especially in these days when houses and flats are built without larders. If you are thinking of buying a new one, make sure it has a decent sized freezer compartment.

Essentials

Openers

Corkscrews and Bottle Openers: I know Molly will laugh at me for putting this first but somebody has to make sure we get our priorities right and frankly there is nothing much more frustrating than a bottle or indeed a container of any sort that one can't open.

We have a splendid corkscrew with a fancy handle made from vine wood which was used so much that the tip eventually succumbed to metal fatigue and broke off. We still keep it for emergencies but it does require a fair amount of strength and to pull some of the artificial corks in use nowadays you need arms like an all-in wrestler. Try, instead, as we have, a metal opener with two handles which rise as you screw into the cork and on which you simply press down to extract it from the bottle.

These don't require anything like the strength of an ordinary corkscrew but Molly's mother, who was very small, still found them difficult so we bought her one of the type which uses a hollow needle to inject air through the cork and is guaranteed not to harm the wine.

Bottle Opener: These are fairly straightforward but, bearing in mind that we hope to be drinking as well as cooking at a hundred, we have one with an extra long handle which, while not long enough to move the world, makes opening beer and mineral water bottles a snip and which also has a metal tongue for making holes in cans that don't have ring pulls. It can also come in handy for pulling those tough ring pulls that seem to have been made expressly to deny the contents of the can to people of ordinary strength and dexterity.

Can Opener: A well fixed wall-mounted opener is a real boon – a must in fact. They are a lot easier to operate than the hand held variety, some of which are positively lethal, although if you have a favourite that works reasonably well you could keep it in reserve for emergencies and for picnics. Electric openers are fine if you can afford one and well worth the money if you find it difficult to operate even the wall-mounted hand operated type.

Screw Top Bottle Opener: This is just a large pair of sturdy metal pincers which enable you to exert enough pressure to open impossible items like sauce bottles and jam jars. They are worth their weight in large denomination notes but don't despair if you haven't got a pair; just invert the jar or bottle into an inch or so of hot water and then use a cloth to twist off the expanded lid.

Cutters and Choppers

Knives: You probably already have several favourites but a few really sharp knives are essential and it's a good idea either to keep them in a separate drawer or on a wall-mounted magnetic rack. You can collect them one by one but priorities should be a bread knife, a carving knife, a couple of small sharp kitchen knives and a palette knife for lifting biscuits off a baking tray.

Scissors: A strong comfortable pair kept solely for kitchen use is incredibly useful not only for cutting up herbs, snipping the fins off fish and cutting up foil and greaseproof paper but also for opening all those packets, sachets and cartons with optimistic instructions to 'tear along the dotted line'.

Graters: Some form of grater is essential; you might prefer a set of graters with a small interchangeable handle or an attachment to a food mixer or processor, but for quick everyday use the old fashioned four-sided grater is the easiest to use and the easiest to clean. It's also the cheapest.

Measures

A set of scales is useful, plus a glass measuring jug that gives you fluid ounce measurements as well as imperial and metric volumes. And one of the best small presents we have been given was a set of plastic measuring spoons hanging from a ring.

Pans

This is very much a matter of choice. Cast-iron ware, although excellent for cooking, is much too heavy to be recommended except for frying pans. Aluminium pans are very hard wearing and long lasting – we have a couple of these but we have found the good quality non-stick pans excellent, especially for sauces, and we keep a small non-stick frying pan specially for pancakes. Try to make sure that whatever you use sits safely and firmly on your cooker. It's no use giving away your heavy pans and replacing them with lightweights which are easily knocked over or overbalance if they are slightly off centre.

Baking Tools

Absolute essentials are a rolling pin, some good solid baking sheets for biscuits, scones and home-made rolls, large patty tins, bread tins — we find the non stick variety invaluable for both bread and cakes — pie plates for tarts and pies. Funnily enough this is one instance of the old fashioned equipment bring by far the best, as nothing cooks the pastry more evenly than enamelled pie plates.

Mixing Bowls: If you switch to a plastic bowl from one of the heavier pottery ones don't forget to stand it on a damp cloth, otherwise it will shoot off the worktop when you are mixing vigorously.

Mixers

We have two very tiny balloon whisks which cost only a few shillings and are useful for beating egg whites or for lightly beating in cream. Our small electric hand whisk can be used anywhere and is in constant use, as is our blender which is used almost daily for blending soups, sauces, pureés, ice creams, breadcrumbs and making caster sugar from granulated. We don't have a food processor but our friends Dorothy and Ted find theirs invaluable because it takes all the hard work out of kneading bread and as they bake three times a week this was becoming a chore. It also does all the work of a mincer and shreds and slices in no time. After resisting for some time they reluctantly accepted a food processor as a diamond wedding present and now they wouldn't be without it.

Timer

Very useful if, like me, you are inclined to daydream. Neither of us will ever learn but it is really no use asking your partner to let you know when ten minutes or half an hour has gone by, because it's all too easy to stay in the garden or get involved in a book or a TV programme until the first whiff of burning floats through from the kitchen.

There are many other items which some people regard as essentials and others wouldn't have in the kitchen. Among these are:

Pressure Cooker

The retired cook's friend; cooks stews, casseroles, soups, pulses, vegetables, jams and preserves in very little time which can save a fortune on fuel. They do tend to be heavy though, so make sure yours has a firm handle on each side.

Dishwasher

Molly is a card-carrying Luddite which, while it has in the past prevented us from taking immediate advantage of new technology, has also prevented us from making one or two expensive mistakes. Curiously, however, once some gleaming piece of equipment has found its way into the kitchen it doesn't take too long before she is saying that she doesn't know how she ever managed without it. For my money, if you are going to enjoy cooking in retirement a dishwasher, while not essential, is a splendid investment. After all, if you are going to cook for pleasure, as opposed to merely putting food on the table, the chances are that you might be using quite a lot of bowls, tins and pans. This can spoil the fun but with a dishwasher it doesn't matter how many dishes you use.

I was taught to cook by a delightful girl who had a couple of staff in her kitchen, as well as a fair amount of cash, so I tend to be profligate with the bowls and dishes and leave the kitchen looking like a battlefield. Molly learned from her mother who knew how to be both tidy and frugal, so for a long time she said she didn't need and didn't want a dishwasher. However, three days after she went away on some course or other and left me to cope on my own I had a machine installed and we have had one ever since. Now if it broke down it would be a major disaster.

Deep Freeze

This was another item that our resident Luddite 'didn't need'. They were, according to her, a waste of money because people bought vast quantities of jointed carcasses they didn't want and filled shelves with silly cakes and pastries instead of making fresh. They were, she said, just a gimmick to help sell more frozen food. Then we inherited one from a neighbour who was buying a new and larger one and now we honestly don't know how we managed without it. We make sorbets and ice creams, freeze our surplus fruit and vegetables, make a 'pie for the freezer' at the same time as one for dinner.

If you are asked to choose a piece of kitchen equipment as a retirement present this could well be it, or you might consider investing in a second hand one. Don't bother about the odd chip in the enamel but check the seal and do make sure you get some sort of warranty. Uprights cost more to run but we feel they are worth it because it's much easier to get at things and to check what you have in store.

Microwave

We don't have one of these ourselves but many of our elderly relatives find them an invaluable 'extra' for quickly cooking meat or reheating whole meals without any drying up. One aunt freezes a serving of the Sunday roast dinner and uses the microwave to give her an instant roast meal in mid week, while an elderly friend cooks only three times a week and uses her microwave to heat the rest of her meals.

Although some people complain about the quality of baking in a microwave and the fact that a time misjudgement can ruin the food, the people who have really taken time to study the directions and to experiment with the cookers seem to be immediate converts and assure us that the saving in fuel is quite considerable.

It took us ages to realise that for much of the time we now have no one to consider but ourselves and in the case of kitchens this means that whatever works for you − and will continue to work for you in the future − is just fine.

That being said, the main thing is to ensure that all the utensils and ingredients you require frequently are visible or easily reached and that everything you are likely to need is near at hand and not on the top shelf of a high cupboard. In fact unless you are very short of space high cupboards are a dangerous nuisance. If you have to use them, store things in them that you only need once in a blue moon and when you need the article in question use a safely secured stepladder or preferably get a youngster to climb up for you. Never use a chair or a stool. And don't forget that drawers are a lot easier to get into than base cupboards where you have to bend or kneel down to reach in. Wide drawers can hold awkward things like baking tins and those pull out larder fitments with rows of wire baskets are one of the best things I've come across for storing vegetables.

This sort of thing makes sense from a practical point of view – you don't waste anything because you can see all your vegetables at a glance – and is one item you might think of when refurbishing a kitchen.

Another, which I have mentioned earlier, is the high oven which saves all that bending to take out hot dishes which turns a conventional low oven into a contortionist act at best and at worst a rupture trap. And while you are replacing the oven it might make sense to install one of those double ones. The small economical one can be used most of the time, reserving the large one for large-scale baking and cooking for guests.

Safety points include trying to ensure that you have adequate work surfaces, bearing in mind that if your cooking in retirement is going to be enterprising and interesting you will need space to put things down both before and after going in the oven. Of course if you have a galley sized kitchen you will have to adjust your working style accordingly – although any DIY enthusiast can increase your working area by fitting hook-on or fold-down flaps to existing surfaces; but I must confess a weakness for farm house kitchens with large deal tables providing lots of room to put down everything you need to produce a complete dinner, including a cup of tea or a glass of wine for the cook.

Using a Blender

The blender is our favourite among small kitchen appliances and we can't imagine how we managed without it. It stands permanently on a work surface, ready for action, and is in use virtually every day.

At one time its use was generally limited to making drinks and cream soups and it was usually called a liquidiser but it can also be used for chopping, light whisking, making purées and pâtés and the most delectable desserts.

You will find references to a blender in many of the recipes throughout the book but the following examples will give you some idea of its versatility.

(Facing) **Recipes using Frozen Fish Steaks:** Baked in Foil with Fennel, Goujons with Mustard, Fish and Vegetable Terrine

Cream of Parsnip Soup

Preparation time: 5 minutes
Cooking time: 15 minutes

Imperial (Metric)

2 tablespoons vegetable oil
2 medium parsnips
1 large onion
1½ pints (850 ml) stock or stock cube
    and water
seasoning to taste
chopped fresh basil or parsley for
    garnish

American

2 tablespoons vegetable oil
2 medium parsnips
1 large onion
3¾ cups stock or stock cube and water
seasoning to taste
chopped fresh basil or parsley for
    garnish

1. Heat oil in a large pan. Peel and finely chop onion and parsnip and sauté in oil over low heat for four minutes.
2. Add the stock or water and stock cube, bring to the boil and simmer for ten minutes.
3. Season, whizz for 30 seconds in blender, reheat for one minute, sprinkle with garnish and serve with triangles of toast or hot rolls.

Variations
1. Stir in 4 tablespoons hummus at stage 3 until it melts.
2. Add a grated carrot at stage 1.
3. Add 2 tablespoons chopped parsley before blending.

Quick Watercress Soup

Preparation time: 5 minutes
Cooking time: 8 minutes

Imperial (Metric)

2 small bunches watercress
1¼ pints (710 ml) water
1 chicken or vegetable stock cube
1 tablespoon (25 g) instant potato
black pepper, salt
2 tablespoons cream

American

2 small bunches watercress
3 cups water
1 chicken or vegetable stock cube
1 tablespoon instant potato
black pepper, salt
2 tablespoons cream

1. Put everything in the blender except the cream. Whizz for 30 seconds, stop then repeat.

(Facing) **Flans:** Spinach and Cheese Flan, Onion with Mushroom Flan

2. Pour into a large pan and gently heat. Simmer for five minutes, adjust seasoning and serve. Swirl a little cream into each bowl.

Variations
1. Replace watercress with ½ lb (225 g) frozen spinach or young spinach leaves.
2. Replace instant potato with ½ lb (225 g) (1 cup) of cooked mashed potato.

 # Cream of Mushroom Soup

Preparation time: 5 minutes
Cooking time: 10 minutes

Imperial (Metric)	American
½ lb (225 g) mushrooms	*½ lb mushrooms*
tablespoon cooking oil	*tablespoon cooking oil*
1 small onion	*1 small onion*
tablespoon sherry	*tablespoon sherry*
1½ pints (850 ml) chicken stock or cube and water	*3¾ cups chicken stock or cube and water*
1 clove of garlic	*1 clove of garlic*
tablespoon chopped chives	*tablespoon chopped chives*

1. Chop onion, peel and chop garlic, slice mushrooms and sauté in oil for two minutes.
2. Put into blender with stock cube and most of water. Whizz for 30 seconds.
3. Pour into large pan with rest of stock or water, bring to boil and simmer for eight minutes. Serve with a little sherry swirled in and chives to garnish. This is excellent when served with garlic bread.

Variations
1. Float thinly sliced, lightly fried mushrooms on top.
2. Thicken with a little mashed potato or chick peas at blending stage to make a more substantial soup.

 # Spring Vegetable Soup

Preparation time: 5 minutes
Cooking time: 20 minutes

Imperial (Metric)	American
1 bunch spring onions	*1 bunch scallions*
about 1 lb weight (450 g) spring vegetables, i.e. carrots, celery,	*about 1 lb spring vegetables, i.e. carrots, celery, broccoli,*

broccoli, cauliflower, spinach, peas,
   etc.
1½ pints (850 ml) stock
2 tablespoons cooking oil
2 tablespoons chopped parsley
bay leaf
salt and pepper

cauliflower, spinach, peas, etc.
3¾ cups stock
2 tablespoons cooking oil
2 tablespoons chopped parsley
bay leaf
salt and pepper

1. Coarsely chop vegetables and sauté for five minutes. Blend for 30 seconds with some of the liquid. Pour into pan with rest of the liquid.
2. Bring to the boil, add bay leaf and simmer for 15 minutes. Remove bay leaf. Adjust seasoning and sprinkle with chopped parsley. Serve with crusty bread.

Variations
1. If using garden peas, reserve until simmer stage.
2. Add 2 oz (50 g) (½ cup) grated cheese just before serving.

 # Traditional English Potted Meat

Preparation time: 20 minutes
Cooking time: About three hours

Imperial (Metric)	American
1 lb (450 g) stewing steak	1 lb beef
1 bay leaf	1 bay leaf
water	water
beef stock cube	beef stock cube
salt and pepper	salt and pepper
few drops Worcestershire Sauce	few drops Worcestershire Sauce
2 oz (50 g) butter	¼ cup butter

This takes a long time to cook, so unless you have an Aga-type cooker it's best to make it when the oven is on for baking or slow cooking. Alternatively it's an excellent recipe for a pressure cooker or a slow cooker.

1. Remove all fat and gristle from meat and cut into chunks. Place everything in an ovenproof dish with a pint (570 g) (2½ cups) of water.
2. Cover dish and place in top of oven at 425°F/220°C/Gas Mark 7 for 15 minutes then change dish to bottom of oven for rest of cooking time.
3. Remove from oven, cool slightly then remove bay leaf and blend meat and liquid until smooth. Press into small tubs and cover with melted butter (see next recipe).

 # Old Fashioned Potted Prawns or Shrimps

Preparation time: 15 minutes
Cooking time: 1 minute for butter

Imperial (Metric)

8 oz (225 g) peeled prawns or shrimps
6 oz (175 g) butter
pinch nutmeg
salt and black pepper

American

½ lb peeled prawns
¾ cup butter
pinch nutmeg
salt and black pepper

1. Melt 4 oz (110 g) (½ cup) butter and pour into blender with prawns, nutmeg. Blend until very smooth. Taste and add seasoning. Blend again for five seconds. Press into small pots and place in refrigerator.
2. Melt the rest of the butter, pour through cheesecloth or muslin to remove any sediment and pour over prawns to cover. Return to refrigerator and use within a week.

Flan Fillings

The blender is particularly useful for whisking up flan fillings. We usually bake three cases at a time, cooking them 'blind' for ten mintes, filled with greaseproof paper and dried peas. We keep the dried peas in a closed jar so that we don't try to use them for soup.

 # Onion Flan

Preparation time: 15 minutes (using prepared flan case)
Cooking time: 35 to 40 minutes

Imperial (Metric)

2 medium onions
2 eggs
2 oz (50 g) plain flour
2 tablespoons milk
2 medium mushrooms
tablespoon cooking oil

American

2 medium onions
2 eggs
½ cup all purpose flour
2 tablespoons milk
2 medium mushrooms
tablespoon cooking oil

1. Chop onions and sauté lightly in oil for five minutes, then put into blender with all ingredients except mushrooms. Whizz for 30 seconds.
2. Pour into flan case and arrange finely sliced mushrooms in pattern on top. Bake at 375°F/190°C/Gas Mark 5 for about 35 minutes.

If you are baking several flans, transfer the lower ones to the top for an extra few minutes after the first one is ready.

Variations

1. Replace onions and mushrooms by 4 oz (110 g) (1 cup) chopped spinach and

4 oz (110 g) (1 cup) grated cheese. Blend and cook as before.
2. Replace onions and mushrooms by drained 7 oz (200 g) canned tuna or salmon. Blend as before and sprinkle top with 1 tablespoon chopped chives.

Desserts

You can make delicious ice creams and sorbets very easily with a blender and you will find a large number of recipes for these later in the book; but just to give you an example of how easy they are here are a couple of our favourites.

Orange Ice Cream

Preparation time: 10 minutes
Cooking time: none

Imperial (Metric)

2 small oranges
3 eggs
1 tablespoon clear honey
7 fl oz (200 ml) double cream

American

2 small oranges
3 eggs
1 tablespoon clear honey
¾ cup heavy cream

1. Peel oranges, remove pips and pith. Divide into segments.
2. Blend until smooth. Add cream and blend for few seconds. Whisk eggs and honey together until thick.
3. Fold egg mixture into orange cream, pour into container and freeze.

Strawberry Sorbet

Preparation time: 10 minutes
Cooking time: 10 minutes

Imperial (Metric)

1 lb (450 g) fresh strawberries
6 oz (175 g) caster sugar
½ pint (275 ml) water
juice of 1 lemon
2 egg whites

American

1 lb fresh strawberries
1 cup caster suagr
1⅓ cups water
juice of 1 lemon
2 egg whites

1. Whizz strawberries to a purée in blender.
2. Dissolve sugar slowly in water, bring to boil and simmer for ten minutes.
3. Take off heat and stir in purée, add lemon juice, pour into a bowl and allow to cool.
4. Pour into polythene container and place in freezer until frozen around the edges, then remove from freezer, whisk egg whites until stiff, scrape mixture and

whites of egg into blender and whizz for ten seconds. Refill polythene container and replace in freezer with lid on. Leave at least four hours, preferably overnight.

3

Meal Stretchers
&
Money Stretchers

We all have to eat and most of us like to eat at specified times which, strangely enough, is good news for retired people and those who, like ourselves, work largely from home.

The fact is that once you no longer have to get up at a certain time every working morning and are no longer forced to live your life in accordance with an inflexible schedule, the skeletal routine of breakfast, lunch and dinner or supper, fleshed out with coffee and tea breaks, is useful and perhaps even essential.

Of course this doesn't mean that you have to eat every meal on the dot of the appointed time, as you probably once had to do, and in fact there can be something deliciously wicked in having a meal an hour or so later than usual, simply because you spent longer than you intended in a friendly pub or, for that matter, a library or a department store.

That being said, it makes sense to eat regularly and, in our case, we have discovered that it provides an element of stability in a life style which might otherwise become more than a little unstructured. Again, especially if you live alone, eating regularly can help you to live longer by forming habits which help to ensure that you eat — even at times when you may not feel like it.

The trouble is that although cooking is great fun it stops being fun for most of us if we have to do it day in day out whether we want to or not, and it can become a chore rather than a pleasure, which is something to be avoided at all costs.

Fortunately, the fact that we have to eat every day doesn't mean that we have to cook every day, unless we want to, and as a life long sufferer from ergasophobia — or a morbid fear of work — I'm happy to say that cooks have devoted a lot of thought to the question of making life easier by using short cuts and by creating 'elastic' dishes that can be stretched to several meals.

One of the simplest ways to stretch a dish is to cook twice as much as you need and keep the rest for later. This used to be a bit boring as you didn't want the same meal two days running, but the idea has becomes much more attractive since the advent of deep freezers and microwave ovens made it possible to keep complete meals for weeks and to reheat them in minutes.

As we mentioned in the previous chapter, many people, for example, who enjoy a traditional Sunday lunch of meat and two veg now pop half the meal into the freezer and have the treat of a second Sunday lunch in the middle of the week without cooking at all.

Of course not everyone has a freezer and a microwave to fall back on and besides, although they can be extremely useful in as much as they give you a chance to enjoy your own cooking without any of the trouble, they are not the complete answer.

I first became interested in cooking, as opposed to eating, while serving with a small army unit in northern Germany just after the end of World War II, when our Mess was in a large villa and our kitchen staff consisted of a German cook called Ella and her assistants, one Polish and one Lithuanian. What these three ladies were able to do with army rations, supplemented by a little judicious bartering of tinned food for fresh, was little short of miraculous and it was they, for example, who introduced me to the virtues of the infinitely expandable compote.

In those days the army was very fond of prunes, which meant that prunes and custard featured heavily on the menus of most military establishments. In our Mess, together with that other old standby dried apple rings, they frequently went into the compote, along with sultanas, the remains of any stewed or tinned fruit used in other dishes, plus any drops left in brandy, sherry or port bottles and any available fruit juice. The result, which featured at every breakfast, along with the traditional bacon and eggs, was a constantly changing delight which, as I came to appreciate, needed very little work on the part of the cook and not much expenditure either.

We often keep one going several days, particularly in the soft fruit season when there are sometimes a few loganberries or redcurrants and a handful of gooseberries ready before the main crop. Stewed with a little sugar if necessary, mixed with a few raisins or grated apple and any available pieces of tinned fruits, and kept liquid by adding the ends of wine or pure fruit juices such as apple or orange, the compote can be served on its own or mixed with breakfast cereal. It also makes a good hot pudding with the addition of a crumble topping.

Ella and her cooks also kept witches' brew stockpots bubbling on the stove, containing splendid smelling bases of meat or chicken bones which somehow became instant soup with the addition of a few vegetables and some of their superb dumplings.

Later, as a busy but impoverished junior reporter, I learned to appreciate the value of stockpots and compotes, even though I could rarely afford to be quite so lavish about keeping them topped up.

I usually managed to keep at least one stockpot going and found the strong taste of ham bones and bacon pieces, often scrounged from the butcher for my imaginary dog, made a great starter for hearty soups — especially those featuring split peas or lentils — while a beef stock was equally nourishing and even more versatile.

Always simmer the ingredients for stock, skim off any scum that rises to the surface — use a large spoon and skim right across the pan — and if you are using marrowbones or neck of mutton it's best to allow the stock to cool so that you can lift off the solidified fat.

Here is a simple recipe for stock, very similar to one of Ella's.

 # Beef or Ham Stock

Preparation time: 5 minutes
Cooking time: 4 hours

Imperial (Metric)	American
3 lb (1.5 kg) beef or ham bones	*3 lb beef or ham bones*
2 onions, chopped roughly	*2 onions, chopped roughly*
2 sliced carrots	*2 sliced carrots*
1 bay leaf	*1 bay leaf*
salt and pepper	*salt and pepper*
pinch of dried herbs	*pinch of dried herbs*
about 5 pints (3 litres) of water	*about 5 pints of water*

1. Bring everything to the boil, remove scum and lower the heat.
2. Simmer very gently for at least four hours.
3. Cool a little then strain into a clean pan. Allow to cool completely and remove fat.

The stock is then ready for use. Nowadays, if you have a freezer you will find it useful to freeze small amounts of the concentrated stock in containers, ready for use as required. Otherwise you must bring the stock to the boil daily.

If you have a pressure cooker you will need only 2 pints of water (just over a litre) and will need only 40 minutes at 15 lb pressure. This will make a very concentrated stock.

You can make an incredible variety of soups out of any vaguely compatible ingredients, as well as trying well tested recipes. Even with the same ingredients you can make two entirely different soups simply by altering the consistency. The easiest way to try this is to make a good vegetable soup, finely chopping your selection of vegetables — always using at least one onion for flavour — and adding seasoning to taste. Use half of the soup and next day liquidise or blend the remainder with a little milk to make a cream soup. The flavour will be quite different and you can vary it even more by using one of my favourite tricks of rinsing out almost empty sauce bottles with a little milk and adding to the soup. Add a sprinkling of chopped parsley or chives and, with a hunk of bread, you have a satisfying meal.

Dumplings turn a soup into an even more substantial meal and are another useful item when feeding unexpected guests or for stretching meals for yourself. They are very quickly made and I've yet to meet anyone who doesn't like them.

 # Dumplings

Preparation time: 10 minutes
Cooking time: 25 minutes

Imperial (Metric)	**American**
4 oz (110 g) self-raising flour	*1 cup self-rising flour*
2 oz (50 g) shredded suet	*2 oz shredded suet*
salt and black pepper	*salt and black pepper*

1. Mix the flour and seasoning in a bowl. Very lightly mix in the suet.
2. Add just enough cold water to make a stiff dough. Shape into 8 or 10 dumplings.
3. When the soup is ready, bring to the boil and drop dumplings in. Cover and cook for 25 minutes. Make sure the soup remains just above boiling.

If you have no suet you can substitute grated block margarine and you can also add various ingredients to the dumplings as long as they don't clash with the flavour of the soup.

Variations
1. Add tablespoon chopped chives or parsley at stage 1.
2. Add tablespoon grated cheese at stage 1.
3. Add small finely grated onion and 2 or 3 finely chopped mushrooms at same time as suet.

All these dumplings are excellent as additions to hotpots or stews, in which case you can drain off sufficient liquid to cook the dumplings separately and then place them and the liquid on top of the serving dish.

I have to confess that I have had the odd failure with my throw-in-anything soups, usually as a result of trying to be too clever by adding too many new ingredients at once instead of making each addition slowly and tasting as I went along, but the disasters have been few and far between. In fact the only real disadvantage of this method of soup making is that when guests praise your efforts and ask for the recipe you can sometimes appear ungracious because you simply do not know. I usually tell them it's an old Latvian recipe, the secret of which I have sworn never to reveal.

As with compotes you can often try a controlled experiment when adding new ingredients by taking out half a cupful of your basic soup and adding minute quantities of a chopped herb or spice to see if you like it.

Using the 'elastic' food method is extremely economical and very satisfying as you can create any number of splendid soups from a simple basic recipe made either with home-made stock or with stock cubes, which we often use.

You can also stretch and improve bought soups, both the tinned and packet variety, most of which can be turned into gourmet dishes with very little effort.

It's a matter for your own conscience whether or not you acknowledge the contribution of Messrs Campbell or Heinz but their products, especially the tins of concentrated soups, are so handy they deserve a bit of credit.

Almost every soup can be improved out of recognition by the addition of a drop or two of sherry, cream or both. You don't need lashings of either and anything from a virtually homeopathic drop of sherry to a teaspoonful is usually enough. The one exception is green pea soup, the thick sort made with dried peas, onions and ham stock, which is absolutely superb with a really generous swirl of cream and a good slug of Harvey's best.

Another foolproof method of improving bought soup is to add some of the ingredients which are in the soup already. Try, for example, slicing a large mushroom fairly thinly into your next tin of mushroom soup or adding fried onion rings to your onion soup.

Even packet soups can be given the 'added ingredient' treatment and here, for example, is a gourmet dish for two. Heat up a packet of asparagus soup, add zests of lemon peel while simmering and serve with a crusty roll. Voilà – Soupe aux Asperges avec Zestes de Citron!

Zests are those strips of thin peel – the outside only – which you pare off with a potato peeler or a special little tool. Try both orange and lemon – orange with carrot soup is terrific – but try to use up the rest of the fruit within a couple of days.

One great thing about cooking in retirement is that you don't have to make three course lunches and dinners every day of your life if you don't want to. We find, for instance, that most soups, especially home-made ones, will make a complete meal with the addition of bread and a small dessert.

Dumplings, as I have mentioned, turn soup into a substantial meal but you could also add pasta – the shells or bows are best – or alternatively serve the soup with croutons or garlic bread. The croutons are simply small squares of bread, shallow fried until golden brown and served hot on top of the bowls of soup.

For garlic bread we usually take a long 'bloomer' type loaf, slice it, rub garlic and butter on both sides of each slice, wrap in foil and heat in a medium oven for 20 minutes.

Once you've got the hang of 'stretching' meals you can use the idea to economise and to save work on all sorts of dishes, as we'll be indicating in other sections.

However, there are one or two things which, like soups, are so elastic that they are worth considering separately just for their stretching properties.

Rice

If you are cooking rice it pays to cook a little extra as you can make it stretch to three or four meals at least.

Say that you have made some plain rice to go with a curry; you could use what you have left to make a rice salad, rice fritters and quick rice pudding, even stretching the rice pudding itself still further by adding fruit or jam.

To show what we mean, here are a few recipes.

 # Rice Salad

Preparation time: 20 minutes for salad
Cooking time: 20 minutes for rice

Rice

Imperial (Metric)	American
8 oz (225 g) rice (uncooked)	*1 cup uncooked rice*
1 dessertspoon olive or vegetable oil	*1 dessertspoon olive or vegetable oil*
1 pint water (570 ml)	*2½ cups water*
salt	*salt*

1. Heat the oil gently in deep saucepan, add rice and stir.
2. Add the boiling water and a little salt, stir again then put on lid.
3. Turn down heat to lowest, simmer and leave for 15 minutes.

The rice is then ready to use.

Salad

Imperial (Metric)	American
2 spring onions	*2 scallions*
4 mushrooms	*4 mushrooms*
tablespoon chopped red pepper	*tablespoon chopped red pepper*
2 tablespoons chopped raisins	*2 tablespoons chopped raisins*
4 oz (110 g) prawns or tuna	*½ cup prawns or tuna*
4 oz (110 g) cooked peas, or corn	*½ cup cooked peas, or corn*

1. Thinly slice mushrooms and spring onions, add the rest of the ingredients and mix with one third of rice. Tip into large salad bowl.
2. Mix with dressing made from:

Dressing

Imperial (Metric)	American
2 tablespoons olive oil	*2 tablespoons olive oil*
2 teaspoons wine vinegar	*2 teaspoons wine vinegar*
grated rind of ½ lemon	*grated rind of ½ lemon*
salt and black pepper	*salt and black pepper*

Put all the ingredients in a screw top bottle and shake thoroughly before using.

Serve with lemon wedges and brown bread.

Cover the remainder of the rice and refrigerate. Next day use half of the remainder to make rice fritters.

 # Rice Fritters

Preparation time: 15 minutes
Cooking time: 20 minutes

1. The amount of ingredients depends on the amount of rice you use. Put cooked rice in a mixing bowl, add a beaten egg, a grated onion and a few chopped mushrooms. Add enough flour to bind the mixture.
2. Drop spoonsful into hot oil, turn after two minutes and cook other side until golden, pressing down with spatula to flatten. Keep hot while you cook the rest. Serve with ketchup or soy sauce.

The final portion of rice can be used for a quick pudding by simmering with a tablespoon of sugar and just enough milk to cover. Add a few raisins or a little apple purée to add flavour, or simply serve with a good teaspoonful of marmalade or strawberry jam.

Marmalade and Jam

Marmalade and jam are tremendously helpful in stretching foods. They can be mixed into plain yoghurt to provide a quick dessert or made into delicious fried sandwiches. Make a jam or marmalade sandwich, cut off crusts and cut into four. Dip in flour and water batter (see p. 15), deep fry until golden, drain well and serve with caster sugar sprinkled on top.

You will also find that marmalade adds taste to boring frozen chicken if you use it as you would mint jelly or apple sauce. Choose the strong flavoured chunky orange variety for preference.

We like a teaspoonful added to orange jelly (jello) and you might also try strawberry jam mixed in a strawberry jelly. You can vary jellies tremendously by adding fruit such as grated apple to raspberry jelly or, during the season, setting fresh strawberries in jelly.

Potatoes

Potatoes are marvellously elastic, especially mashed potatoes and it is worthwhile boiling a few more than you need since the remainder can so easily be made into another meal.

You can simply mash them with a little grated onion and cheese and heat in a solid frying pan until the bottom goes lovely and crusty — keep lifting the sides until you get lots of golden brown bits — or you can use them to make potato cakes, fish cakes or the topping to a cottage pie.

 # Potato Cakes

Preparation time: 10 minutes

Cooking time: 30 minutes

Imperial (Metric)

8 oz (225 g) mashed cooked potato
8 oz (225 g) self-raising flour
2 tablespoons butter
½ teaspoon salt
3 tablespoons milk

American

1 cup mashed cooked potato
2 cups self-rising flour
2 tablespoons butter
½ teaspoon salt
3 tablespoons milk

These are great family favourites and always seem to go down well with young visitors.

1. Mix flour, salt and butter, then add potato and thoroughly mix together.
2. Add milk to make a very soft dough. You may need a little more milk.
3. Roll out onto a floured board and, using a saucer, cut into large rounds. Mark lightly into farls (triangles) on top of cakes and bake at 425°F/220°C/Gas Mark 7

for about 30 minutes. Serve hot with butter. If preferred you can cut into 3 inch (7.5 cm) rounds before baking.

Variation

If you want potato cakes in a hurry and don't want to put the oven on, it is easy to make a slightly different version, using a heavy pan or griddle.

There are both Irish and Scottish recipes for these but if you haven't already got a good family one this is one we have been using for years.

Preparation time: 10 minutes
Cooking time: 6 minutes each batch

Imperial (Metric)

2 lb (900 g) mashed cooked potato
2 tablespoons bacon fat (or melted
*   butter)*
about 4 tablespoons flour
pinch salt

American

4 cups mashed cooked potato
2 tablespoons bacon fat (or melted
*   butter)*
about 4 tablespoons flour
pinch salt

1. Work all ingredients together well, adding a bit more flour if the potatoes are at all waxy.
2. Roll out on a floured surface to about ½ inch (1 cm) thick. Mark out large circles and cut into triangles. Heat a greased griddle or heavy frying pan.
3. Prick the potato cakes and fry for about three minutes each side.

A couple of these with a rasher of bacon make a very satisfying breakfast or supper dish. They also keep well in a tightly closed tin for several days and can be quickly reheated either in the frying pan or the bottom of the oven; but they are also delicious cold with a little butter.

 Potato Patties

Preparation time: 10 minutes
Cooking time: 10 minutes per batch

Imperial (Metric)

4 oz (110 g) minced or chopped cooked
*   meat*
1 small onion, grated
8 oz (225 g) mashed cooked potato
beaten yolk of egg
salt and pepper
vegetable oil for shallow frying
little flour

American

½ cup minced or chopped cooked meat
1 small onion, grated
1 cup mashed cooked potato
beaten yolk of egg
salt and pepper
vegetable oil for shallow frying
little flour

These economical little patties made from leftovers are one of Molly's mother's recipes; they come from the days when it was roast beef on Sunday, cold meat on

Monday and anything else that could be devised for the rest of the week.

1. Mix all ingredients together, form into cakes with floured hands, flatten and roll in flour.
2. Fry in shallow, hot fat for about five minutes each side.

Variations
1. Substitute 4 oz (110 g) (1 cup) grated cheese for meat and continue as above. Serve with tomato sauce.
2. Substitute 4 oz (110 g) (¾ cup) cooked baked beans or chick peas for meat and continue as above. Serve with onion or tomato sauce.

Pasta

Many pastas are useful for stretching ingredients. Add milk, sugar and a few raisins to a little cooked macaroni and heat for an instant if not very exciting pudding. This is particularly useful if, like me, you invariably cook more than you need when making macaroni cheese. For years, as soon as I realised how much of the stuff I'd cooked, I used to add all the cheese in the house and still finish up with a giant vat of pasta, tasting only vaguely of cheese. Now I measure it and use only as much of the cooked macaroni as I need, and save any small amounts of pasta left to use in a pudding or to add to a soup or salad.

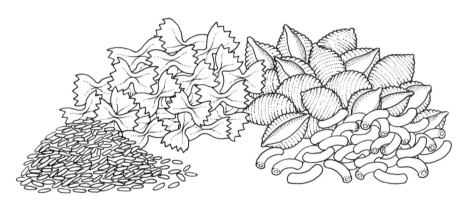

 ## Macaroni Cheese

Preparation time: 15 minutes
Cooking time: 30 minutes

Imperial (Metric)
8 oz (225 g) macaroni
½ pint (275 ml) milk
¼ pint (150 ml) single cream
teaspoon cornflour
½ lb (225 g) grated tasty cheese
*   (Cheddar)*

American
1½ cups dry macaroni
1⅓ cups milk
just over ½ cup light cream
teaspoon cornstarch
2 cups grated cheese
1 egg, beaten

1 egg, beaten
tablespoon chopped fresh parsley or
  teaspoon mixed dried basil and
  thyme (optional)

tablespoon chopped fresh parsley or
  teaspoon mixed dried basil and
  thyme (optional)

This is a version of macaroni cheese which seems to work every time. It makes four portions and I find that if you use only half, the rest is excellent next day, mixed with a beaten egg and an extra ounce of cheese and fried in a heavy, lightly greased frying pan until brown and bubbly.

1. Cook the macaroni for ten minutes in plenty of boiling water. It should be al dente — firm in the centre. Drain and keep on one side.
2. Combine milk, cream — or extra milk if you have no cream — and herbs. Mix the cornflour (cornstarch) with a little of the mixture until it forms a smooth paste, then return to the mixture.
3. Stir in most of the cheese and the beaten egg, then add salt and pepper and the macaroni. Turn into an ovenproof casserole, sprinkle with the remaining cheese and bake in a hot oven 400°F/200°C/Gas Mark 6 for 20 minutes.

When cooking lasagne it's a good tip to put a tablespoon of oil in the boiling water and to lower the sheets of pasta one at a time into the water. This will prevent the sheets from sticking, although if you are cooking a large batch for a family meal it's probably best to do it in two stages. Use long handled tongs to separate after draining.

Although meat is usually included in many lasagne and spaghetti recipes, they are very tasty with just a combination of onions, tomatoes and cheese, with perhaps a few chopped mushrooms for additional flavour, or a slice of cooked bacon, chopped small. You can experiment with pasta, adding small quantities of different herbs and chopped vegetables until you concoct a particularly enjoyable dish which then becomes your own special recipe. But do write down the results of your inventions so that you can repeat your success.

When it comes to puddings, ice cream is usefully elastic and well worth buying in quantity if you have a freezer. There are very good bargains in the plain vanilla variety which you can then improve on.

In the section on home-made ice creams and sorbets we'll be looking at some of the splendid frozen desserts that Molly makes — and the one I'm allowed to make only for dinner parties because it's too expensive for ordinary meals — but, for the moment, it's worth noting that plain vanilla ice cream can be enlivened simply by adding a spoonful of jam, a handful of chopped nuts or raisins or a crumbled bar of flaky chocolate. Mix thoroughly in a bowl and serve in scoops, decorated with a few nuts. You could also try sprinkling on a few grains of coffee or the ubiquitous zests of lemon or orange.

If you happen to have a spoonful of brandy or sherry lying around, soak some sultanas in it overnight and use them with vanilla ice.

The great thing about making food stretch like this is that although you are saving money you are not really using 'left-overs' which sounds a bit yucky but engaging in culinary planning — which is smart. That being the case, it is as well to plan to make things you like. It sounds absurd but most of us have hangups when

(Facing) **Summer Harvest from the Garden**

it comes to food and it takes a conscious effort on occasions to remember that we no longer have to eat up every morsel on our plate.

Do try any of the recipes in this book that you find interesting – even the ones using ingredients you have always disliked – your tastes may have changed since you last tasted the stuff under protest, or the recipe may make it tastier than you remember. If you still can't stand it then give it the elbow because now that you've retired you don't have to please anyone but yourself – and your partner if you have one.

I mention this because my mother, an excellent plain cook who fed us well during six years of wartime rationing with no recourse to the Black Market, had a thing about apples and custard. Not that there was anything wrong with her apples and custard, you understand, but after the third or fourth time in succession I had had enough.

Molly, who saw the same dessert coming to the table whenever she visited, assumed that apples and custard were a family weakness and accordingly served them up fairly often after our marriage; it was some time before I realised that I no longer had to eat them and could indeed suggest that once every couple of months would be quite often enough for this particular dish.

Apples as such are very versatile and you might like to try, for example, a few meals based on baked potatoes and baked apples. Don't put the oven on specially for these; they can be tucked in on a lower shelf when you are baking. 375°F/190°C/Gas Mark 5 will cook a large apple in about 40 minutes. Baked potatoes at this temperature get a nice crusty skin in about 1½ to 2 hours. Although both the apples and the potatoes are delicious straight from the oven they are equally good next day. Serve the baked apple cold with a little ice cream or cream and try halving the potatoes, scooping out the middle and mashing thoroughly with 1 oz grated cheese and a teaspoonful of milk. Pile back in cases and brown under grill. You can add bits of cooked bacon, grated onion and any number of variations while you can vary the baked apples by trying a similar method. Scoop out the middle, beat with a little plain yoghurt, pile back in the case and sprinkle with nutmeg. Or mix the apple pulp with a teaspoonful of sherry or cider, sprinkle with a teaspoonful of brown sugar and pop under the grill until the sugar starts to melt.

You can make an excellent meal of a baked potato and a baked apple, both of which have been cooked as oven 'fillers'.

Apple rings are a favourite during the Bramley season although we have also found dessert apples fry well too. Simply wash, core and slice the apples – we don't peel them unless the skin is pitted – then fry the thin slices in bacon fat and serve with bacon and fried bread.

Stewed apple makes an excellent pancake filling, especially with a little nutmeg dusted on top; and if you have a freezer it's a good idea to use surplus apples to make purée which you can store either in small bags or containers. We store the best apples in the garage in old drawers and trays but try to use up all the rest for purée. Just a little stirred into yoghurt, curd cheese or ice cream, with perhaps a few raisins and a touch of brown sugar, can make a dessert that will stretch from one to a large number of guests.

Apple fritters are easily made and have the advantage of being interchangeable as both a savoury dish and as a pudding.

(Facing) **Soups:** Watercress Soup with Cream, Tomato Soup with Sherry, Carrot, Leek and Orange Soup

 # Apple Fritters

Preparation time: 15 minutes
Cooking time: 5 minutes per batch

Imperial (Metric)	American
2 large apples	*2 large apples*
For batter:	*For batter:*
4 oz (110 g) self-raising flour	*1 cup self-rising flour*
½ teaspoon salt	*½ teaspoon salt*
just over ¼ pint (150 ml) water	*just over ½ cup water*
vegetable oil for deep frying	*vegetable oil for deep frying*

1. Peel, core and thinly slice apples. Whisk water into flour and salt until smooth — an easy way to ensure that your batter is lump free is to put flour and salt in a basin then hold it under a just dripping tap (faucet) and stir like mad until you get a creamy batter.
2. Dip slices of apple in batter and drop carefully, half a dozen at a time, in very hot deep oil. When golden brown, after about five minutes, lift out and drain on absorbent paper. Keep hot until all are done.
3. Serve as a dessert sprinkled with caster sugar and a scoop of ice cream if liked.
4. Serve with pork chop, sausages or hot cheese pasty. They are also delicious with sweet and sour sauce as a side dish to a Chinese meal.

This quantity serves four for a dessert or as a savoury 'stretcher'.

Bread

We'll be discussing cooking for invalids later on in the book but as far as I'm concerned one thing I can almost always eat, no matter how rough I feel, is bread and milk made with buttered bread, sugar and hot milk. It just slides down — but take care because it can get very hot in the pan and could easily burn the throat you are trying to take care of.

If you have any left you can always turn it into a sort of bread pudding the next day by throwing in a few sultanas and some squares of freshly buttered bread on top, spread with marmalade before browning in the oven.

In fact bread is a pretty elastic ingredient altogether and unless it has mould growing on it, can usually be rescued even when stale. We break up any hard bits and grind them for breadcrumbs in the blender; if you don't have one you can put the bread in a plastic bag and crush with a heavy rolling pin. Store the breadcrumbs in an airtight jar. Incidentally, if we want breadcrumbs in large quantity we buy yesterday's bread at half price from our local baker. People who find new bread indigestible could find this a regular saving as, unlike French bread, it's not in the least stale when bought next day.

It's worthwhile keeping a spare loaf or two in your freezer, if you have one, especially if you don't live near the shops.

By the way, I didn't realise until it was pointed out to me that it pays to keep your freezer as full as possible because it's cooling the air that costs all the money.

Getting back to bread, use it in summer puddings — you'll find our friend

Dorothy's family recipe on p. 121 — or make croutons or dip slices in a mixture of beaten egg and milk to make eggy bread, fried to a golden brown. And don't forget how easy it is to make fruit crumble which stretches a bit of stewed fruit to a proper pudding. The usual recipe for crumble topping is with flour but we have experimented with soft white breadcrumbs and found that instead of the 40 minutes or so usually needed for the topping to brown, the breadcrumb variety is ready in about 10 minutes.

 # Breadcrumb Topping

Preparation time: 5 minutes
Cooking time: 10 minutes

Imperial (Metric)	American
8 oz (225 g) soft breadcrumbs	*2 cups soft breadcrumbs*
5 oz (150 g) soft brown sugar	*¾ cup soft brown sugar*
3 oz (75 g) soft butter	*3 oz soft butter*

Mix together breadcrumbs and fat until crumbly, then add sugar and combine well. Spread over cooked fruit in pie dish and brown in moderate oven.

If you want to use flour in this recipe, use plain (all purpose) plus 1 level teaspoon baking powder. The crumble will then take about 40 minutes to brown.

Pancakes

Pancakes (see p. 83) are wonderfully versatile for savoury courses or for desserts and the variations are endless — grated cheese and chives, seafood, chopped ham and mustard, etc: then there's apple and nutmeg, crêpe Suzette and the good old favourite lemon and sugar. When you think that a pancake batter made with just one egg can give you about ten pancakes it has to be one of the most economical 'stretchers' we know. Plain pancakes freeze well if divided by rings of greaseproof paper and packed in fours or sixes. Even if you are going to eat them the same day, it is a good idea to make them, say, in the morning and keep them in the refrigerator until you make the filling later in the day, otherwise it is quite a tiring process to make a large batch.

Using some of these 'elastic' ingredients to stretch meals should enable you not only to save money but time as well, when you need to — and to get by with less cooking on the days when you don't feel like it.

4

Growing for the Pot

A crisp lettuce fresh from the garden takes a lot of beating, as does an apple plucked from your own tree or a new potato that's gone from patch to pan to plate in a matter of minutes. For one thing the fresh stuff tastes marvellous and for another, even though the feeling that your own produce is absolutely free is an illusion, it does cost considerably less than anything you can buy in the shops.

Funnily enough, when I was working full time as a staff reporter we had acres of land but a relatively unproductive kitchen garden, and although this was partly due to the harsh Pennine climate the main reason was that we hadn't much time to spare for gardening. Nowadays, with only a city back garden, we produce a tremendous quantity of foodstuff which ensures the total freshness of most of the ingredients we use in our cooking and saves us several pounds a week. In fact we come close to what should be the ideal for the retired cook by using at least one item of food from our garden every single day of the year.

Not that we spend a great deal of time gardening even now — that would be too much like hard work — but we are able to spend enough time digging, sowing watering and picking at the seasons when it is essential to do so.

It's this ability to do what has to be done in the garden just when it needs to be done — like drying and stringing the onions or gathering the plums and having a jam making session — that gives retired people a big advantage over those who have to wait for a day off that is not only fine enough to work outdoors but hasn't been pre-empted by some other activity, like shopping or decorating or escorting the children.

Another advantage is that as a retired person you have time to plan — which is not only half the battle but half the fun of growing your own food — and it's worth remembering that you are growing largely for yourselves, so do plan to grow the fruit and vegetables that you enjoy. If you've always grown long rows of cabbage and broad beans for the family but don't really like them as much as mangetout or globe artichokes or French beans, now is the time to change your gardening habits.

Send off for every gardening catalogue — most of them are free — buy a drawing book and spend some happy hours planning to put food on your table. If you haven't gardened before or have always concentrated on lawns and flowers, you'll find plenty of excellent books in shops and libraries covering most of the things you'll want to grow. You can use them as a basic guide, but the main thing to keep in mind is that it's *your* garden and should be designed with your requirements in mind and no one else's.

Of course not everyone has even a small garden, but there are plenty of things you can grow even if you have only a window box or a couple of plant pots outside the door. And even without those, it is possible to grow miniature tomatoes on your window ledge and mustard and cress on damp tissue.

Plant Pot and Window Box Gardening

Herbs are a first choice for pots, either by the kitchen door or on the window ledge, and two of the most useful are of course chives and parsley, which we manage to keep going throughout the year. Parsley takes a long time to germinate but if you soak the seed in hot water and allow it to dry overnight before sowing, you'll find it will germinate more quickly. We start seeds off in the laundry room near the boiler and as soon as they are showing we move them onto narrow shelves we have fixed across the window. Everything is 'brought on' here until ready to harden off before planting out; but the shelves are also a useful idea for doubling or trebling your growing area if you have no garden.

Chervil and borage are both easy to grow in pots and basil seems to be easy for many people although, to our dismay, it never does particularly well for us. Mint, of course, in its many varieties grows so well that it has to have a large pot of its own. We use it almost daily during the summer − chopped on tomatoes, cooked with peas and potatoes, shredded in salad, made into mint sauce or jelly and finally dried for the first couple of months of winter. After that it loses its taste.

In a 4 foot window box you could plant out eight 'Tom Thumb' lettuce only three inches apart, one 'Salad Bowl' lettuce − the cut and come again loose leaf lettuce − to hang attractively over the end, a couple of cherry-type tomatoes such as 'Tiny Tim', 'Pixie' or the very hardy 'Arctic Cherry', two short rows of radish and round the back edge grow spring onions (scallions) − the Japanese non-bunching variety, such as 'Ishikura' with straight stems, can be harvested over a very long period. We raise them in a small pot then plant them out by making holes in the soil with a knitting needle or pencil and dropping one plant in each. If the window box faces the sun you could also try an aubergine and a pepper plant or a cucumber, as long as you stake them to grow upwards. Always use good compost, feed regularly, water daily and then enjoy the results. As long as you continue to feed the compost you can continue to replace and replenish to keep the window box in continuous use until the frosts.

If you have a glassed in passageway or shed it can be almost as useful as a greenhouse, and even a bit of plastic pegged over pots or window boxes will prolong your growing season.

Small to Medium-sized Garden

Our town garden is 30 feet wide and less than a hundred feet long from back door to fence, and that includes a fair-sized Victorian tiled yard near the house and a garage and some free standing at the far end. In addition, quite a lot of space is taken up by a brick built electricity sub-station.

One way in which Molly has made the remaining space so productive is to use every wall for growing foodstuffs including the house walls, the garage wall, the fence, the long dividing garden walls and (don't tell the South West Electricity Board) the two walls of the sub-station. Only tough resistance on my part has so far discouraged her from farming the roof of the sub-station, together with that of the laundry room.

Of course we have made some provision for flowers at the front of the house, and the tiled yard or patio does away with the need for a lawn as a sitting out spot. Apart from that we have made our garden reasonably good to look at for most of the year by choosing plants, shrubs and trees — especially trees — that are as pleasing to the eye as their fruits are to the taste.

Fruit trees are a marvellous investment; they give you two for the price of one — blossom in spring and a delicious crop later in the year. Our own fruit trees, some of them roughly espaliered to form a dividing hedge, and the soft fruit growing up every available wall produce a wonderful display of blossom and masses of splendidly coloured fruits ranging from the greens, golds, reds and russets of apples and pears to the deep pink loganberries and raspberries, the dark reds of dessert gooseberries and plums and the deep deep purple of the blackcurrants.

Come to think of it though, there's also a lot that's aesthetically pleasing about a really healthy cabbage or the contrasting reds and greens of a good bed of rhubarb, especially if you can imagine just how good they are going to taste.

One thing about being retired is that you should be able to find the time to keep your bushes and plants well fed and watered, and this means that you can afford to plant things much closer together than the gardening books usually advise. We don't mind occasional weeds, especially if they're pretty — and even more especially if they're edible like young dandelion leaves or nettle tops — and while we wage a sporadic war against slugs and woodlice we tolerate most of the other garden creatures, although a little gratitude and moderation on their part wouldn't come amiss.

One word of warning for butterfly lovers — the popular idea of having a wild corner of the garden to encourage butterflies inevitably means that you encourage caterpillars, and while this doesn't matter in a very large garden, it's a different matter in a small one as we found to our cost when a row of broccoli disappeared overnight because some newly hatched caterpillars preferred cultivated vegetables rather than the weeds.

Of course everyone's garden is different but here is how Molly has laid out ours, or rather adapted it from what it was when we came here, and I and our neighbours can vouch for the fact that it works.

One cardinal rule when gardening for the pot is to buy as little as possible — after all, if you are going to spend a lot of money on plants you might just as well buy all your stuff from your friendly greengrocer instead.

When it comes to gardening, cadging is perfectly respectable — most people have surplus plants and cuttings anyway — although I do think that taking an elegant little trowel around as Molly does is carrying things a bit too far. To be fair she does give away loads of her plants and we've also built up quite a collection by swapping or occasionally exchanging home made sweets or jam for plants or garden produce — a topic we'll be returning to later.

Growing for the pot as opposed to growing for Flower Shows and Beautiful

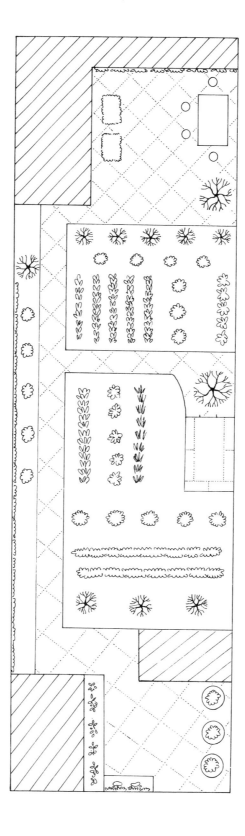

Garden Competitions — although you might also find you enjoy doing that as well — means that the aim is to save as much money and unnecessary work as you can and here again, having time for reconnaissance comes in handy.

Before you start, look at what is already in your garden, decide if it's pulling its weight by providing a good return in tasty food for the amount of space it takes up and, if not, give it the old heave-ho. On the other hand, don't be too eager to dig up everything in sight if you move house and take over a neglected garden. You may find that in your eagerness to clear up you have destroyed a ten-year-old asparagus bed or some prize globe artichokes.

Now is the time to go for a quiet walk around the district looking at other people's gardens, chatting with owners wherever possible to find out what crops grow best. It is amazing how gardeners love to talk gardening — they'd much rather do that than work — and, if you play your cards right, you could well come away with a few cuttings as well as a great deal of useful information. We acquired all our raspberry canes, our super rhubarb bed, cultivated blackberries, logan-berries, some gooseberry bushes and lots of other stuff in this way. In fact the only things we have bought, apart from the grape vine which climbs up the back wall of the house, are the large dessert gooseberry bushes and 'top fruit' trees — apples, pears and plums.

We bought our plum tree from Woolworths and what a bargain it turned out to be with enough plums to eat raw, stew, bottle, make jam, make wine and freeze as well as using them to do a bit of bread casting on the water with friends and neighbours.

We have seven varieties of apples bought from local nurseries over the years, our favourites being a couple of 'Golden Delicious' which grow to cooker size and taste much better than the hard green ones you find in the shops.

Apart from the fruit — which starts with early rhubarb in April and continues with strawberries, red and white currants, loganberries, red, green and yellow gooseberries, blackcurrants, plums, blackberries, pears and then apples from September through to March — we also have vegetables from the garden all year round, popping cloches over winter salad crops such as 'Arctic King' or 'Valdor' lettuce in really severe weather, although we find that corn salad, lamb's lettuce, spinach beet and winter hardy salad onions will usually stand frost and snow. These winter supplies, by the way, are sown in September and are invaluable during the spring 'hungry gap' period before the summer vegetables are ready.

What we don't grow are rows and rows of potatoes. We sometimes grow a couple of plants to provide the newest of new potatoes but most of our new potatoes come from friends with more ground to spare than we have. As for old potatoes, it is easier and more cost effective to buy them by the sack straight from the farm or merchant, usually at a price which is much lower than buying the same spuds a pound at a time. If you don't think you can use up a whole sack, split one with a friend and do the same if you can with any other bulky low cost items, which are simply not worth taking up ground for if the size of your garden is limited.

As for other stuff, I've referred to it before but it really is amazing how some people go on planting row after row of vegetables out of force of habit, long after their families have grown up and left home, or even because most gardening books show vegetables planted in long rows. Now that you have retired you only need to grow for your own needs, for swapping where appropriate and for the occasional guest, so plant short rows, half rows or even quarter rows if that will yield enough produce.

If your garden is too small to have space for a rotation programme according to garden book designs you will have to improvise a little. We find that we never have space for a separate bed for winter greens such as sprouts, kale and sprouting broccoli which have to be planted at least 2 feet apart so we dot three or four about in the salad bed. It doesn't look quite as neat as an allotment row but the plants are very small at this stage and by the time they need more space we will have used the lettuce and radish close to them until gradually, by the end of the summer, the greens will occupy most of the bed.

The following year we move the salad bed and rotate the greens at the same time.

Living as we do in the South-West of England we are fortunate in our climate which is ideal for growing, so much so that in some districts people with wooden walking sticks are said to have to be careful not to leave them in contact with the ground in case they sprout.

Your own reconnaissance walks will tell you what crops are most suited to your particular soil and climate but wherever you live you will probably find some sort of greenhouse invaluable. We have a small metal-framed plastic one which has repaid its cost many times and which Molly uses for raising plants from seed, for bringing on tomatoes before putting them outside and for growing luxuries like melons.

Our garden isn't the tidiest place in the world and as for weeds − most of the time I try to kid people that I'm a wild flower enthusiast, but the garden does produce a lot of good food and that's what growing for the pot is all about.

If your garden is too small or you get hooked on self sufficiency you should perhaps consider renting an allotment, but don't forget that if you do you are moving up to the stage where you may need to spend several hours a week on growing food rather than the odd half hour or so every couple of days as we do.

Allotments

Allotments can also be the answer if you have no access to a garden and if a whole plot is too much for you you can often arrange to share one. It's usually best to divide the plot in two, though, rather than agree to share the work and the produce, as inevitably one of the partners will do more work than the other.

Our friend Ted is a keen gardener who grows his own fruit and vegetables, plus a lot of stuff for his son's family, not to mention us, on a municipal allotment about two miles from home; none of which would be worth mentioning apart from the fact that Ted is well into his eighties.

In fact he and his wife Dorothy, who is also over eighty, seem to have the retirement business well taped, which is why we shall be finding out later in the book how they cope with cooking in retirement and, after twenty years, are still enjoying every minute of it.

You'll find recipes using our garden produce all through this book but here are some of the dishes which we regard as garden 'specials', meaning they are favourites whose main ingredients we grow ourselves.

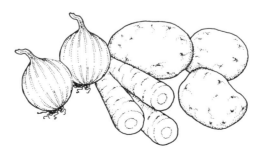

Soups

Carrot, Leek and Orange Soup

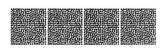

Preparation time: 10 minutes
Cooking time: 25 minutes

Imperial (Metric)

1 lb (450 g) carrots
1 medium leek, chopped
2 tablespoons flour
1 oz (25 g) butter
juice and grated rind of 1 orange
1½ pints (850 ml) stock or cube and
  water
salt and black pepper
chopped chives or parsley

American

1 lb carrots
1 medium leek, chopped
2 tablespoons flour
2 level tablespoons butter
juice and grated rind of 1 orange
3¾ cups stock or cube and water
salt and black pepper
chopped chives or parsley

This soup has a particularly fresh taste and is equally good served hot or cold.

1. Sweat leek in butter for five minutes, then add flour and stir.
2. Add finely chopped carrots and stock and cook over low light for 20 minutes.
3. Add orange juice and rind, liquidise, season with salt and black pepper and serve garnished with chopped chives or parsley.

Tomato Soup

Preparation time: 5 minutes
Cooking time: 15 minutes

Imperial (Metric)

2 lb (900 g) ripe tomatoes
1 large onion, chopped
2 tablespoons wholemeal flour
1 oz (25 g) butter
1 bay leaf
2 teaspoons fresh basil or 1 teaspoon
  dried
1 pint (570 ml) stock or water and cube
¼ pint (150 ml) milk (optional)
salt and black pepper
½ teaspoon Worcestershire Sauce
chopped parsley
tablespoon sherry

American

2 lb ripe tomatoes
1 large onion, chopped
2 tablespoons wholemeal flour
2 level tablespoons butter
1 bay leaf
2 teaspoons fresh basil or 1 teaspoon
  dried
2½ cups stock or water and cube
just over ½ cup milk (optional)
salt and black pepper
½ teaspoon Worcestershire Sauce
chopped parsley
tablespoon sherry

1. Lightly fry onion in butter, add flour and cook for three minutes, stirring frequently.

2. Transfer to large pan and add tomatoes and all other ingredients. Simmer for 10 minutes.
3. Remove bay leaf and add milk if a creamier soup is required. Liquidise, reheat, add a tablespoon of sherry and serve with chopped parsley garnish.

NB Home grown tomatoes usually have soft skins but you may need to sieve the soup before serving if the tomato skins are tough.

Variations
1. Replace basil with fresh chopped mint.
2. Use half stock and half milk and stir in a tablespoon of cream before serving.

We also purée tomatoes and freeze them for use during the winter.

This is very easy and quick to do. Put the tomatoes in a colander. Dip into boiling water to skin them and drop them into a large pan. Simmer them in their own juice for five minutes. Either purée in a blender or push through a sieve, cool and pack in small containers and freeze.

Molly's mother used to make a good tomato sauce with the surplus crop — it keeps well and was always appreciated by her friends.

 # Tomato Sauce

Preparation time: 5 minutes
Cooking time: 65 minutes

Imperial (Metric)	American
2 lb (900 g) ripe tomatoes	*2 lb ripe tomatoes*
2 tablespoons vinegar	*2 tablespoons vinegar*
level tablespoon granulated sugar	*level tablespoon granulated sugar*
½ teaspoon white pepper	*½ teaspoon white pepper*
½ teaspoon salt	*½ teaspoon salt*
pinch cayenne	*pinch cayenne*
1 tablespoon finely chopped onion	*1 tablespoon finely chopped onion*
2 tablespoons water	*2 tablespoons water*
juice of 1 lemon	*juice of 1 lemon*

1. Simmer tomatoes in the water for five minutes. Push through a fine sieve.
2. Put pulp and all other ingredients in large pan. Bring to boil and simmer for an hour, stirring frequently. When cold, bottle and screw tops securely. Keeps for several weeks.

We usually have a splendid crop of sprouting broccoli in spring from our half-dozen plants and find this a very satisfying soup with chunks of home-made bread.

Cream of Broccoli Soup

Preparation time: 10 minutes
Cooking time: 25 minutes

Imperial (Metric)

½ lb (225 g) broccoli spears
stick celery
1 oz (25 g) butter
1 large onion
1½ pints (850 ml) stock
¼ pint (150 ml) milk
pinch nutmeg
1 tablespoon flour
salt and pepper
chopped parsley or lovage

American

½ lb broccoli spears
stick celery
2 level tablespoons butter
1 large onion
3¾ cups stock
just over ½ cup milk
pinch nutmeg
1 tablespoon flour
salt and pepper
chopped parsley or lovage

1. Bring large pan of water to boil, cook broccoli for ten minutes.
2. Chop onion and celery and fry very lightly in butter for ten minutes. Do not brown. Stir in the flour, then add stock and seasonings.
3. Bring to boil, add broccoli and milk. Cool slightly.
4. Blend, reheat and serve sprinkled with nutmeg and chopped parsley or lovage.

Variation
Substitute large bunch of landcress or watercress and medium grated potato for broccoli. Leeks are another of our garden standbys and, as well as serving them in cheese sauce or baked in the oven with a little grated cheese and a layer of thinly sliced potatoes on top, we find them very useful for this winter soup.

Leek and Potato Soup

Preparation time: 10 minutes
Cooking time: 45 minutes

Imperial (Metric)

2 lb (about 1 kg) leeks
1 large potato
1 oz (25 g) butter
1½ pints (850 ml) chicken stock
salt and black pepper
2 tablespoons single cream

American

2 lb leeks
1 large potato
2 level tablespoons butter
3¾ cups chicken stock
salt and black pepper
2 tablespoons light cream

1. Trim leeks, cut through lengthwise, open out and wash thoroughly in cold water.
2. Shred into thin strips, peel and thinly slice the potato. Melt butter and sweat vegetables over low heat for five minutes.
3. Add stock and seasoning and bring to boil. Simmer for 35 minutes.

4. Blend, then reheat. Swirl in cream before serving.

Variation
Omit cream and sprinkle with 2 oz (50g) (½ cup) grated cheese before serving.

Starters

We grow courgettes in large tubs — one inside the greenhouse for an early crop — and marrows for use later in the year and for storing. Because our old brick garden walls play host to so many slugs and snails we lost our marrow plants for years until we tried raising them inside and trailing them up the garden fence. We still have to check the fence for snails each day but we've found this method very successful, using the long green trailing variety. The courgettes are grown in tubs for the same reason and in most years give a splendid crop.

Stuffed Courgettes

Preparation time: 15 minutes
Cooking time: 45 minutes

Imperial (Metric)

6 courgettes about 6 inches (15 cm)
*   long*
2 oz (50 g) white breadcrumbs
2 tablespoons milk
4 oz (110 g) curd cheese
1 clove garlic, crushed or 1 tablespoon
*   chopped onion*
1 egg
sprinkling of dried oregano
2 oz (50 g) grated cheese

American

6 zucchini about 6 inches long
½ cup white breadcrumbs
2 tablespoons milk
½ cup Ricotta cheese
1 clove garlic, crushed or 1 tablespoon
*   chopped onion*
1 egg
sprinkling of dried oregano
½ cup grated cheese

1. Cook courgettes in boiling water for five minutes, drain and cut in half lengthwise. Carefully remove pulp and put shells aside.
2. Chop pulp, mix with all other ingredients except grated cheese. Pile into courgette shells and sprinkle with grated cheese.
3. Place in greased baking dish and bake in oven for 40 minutes at 375F°/190C°/ Gas Mark 5. Serve immediately.

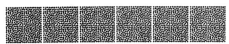 # Leek Puffs

Preparation time: 15 minutes
Cooking time: 20 minutes for the puffs, 10 minutes for the sauce

Imperial (Metric)

*7½ oz (175 g) packet of puff pastry
  (thaw out if frozen)
6 medium leeks, well washed and
  trimmed to about 6 inches (15 cm)
1 egg, beaten*

American

*7½ oz packet of frozen puff pastry
  (thaw out if frozen)
6 medium leeks, well washed and
  trimmed to about 6 inches
1 egg, beaten*

Unless we are making lots of these for a party we always use frozen puff pastry for this recipe, otherwise it's very time consuming for a starter although it's very easy to make.

1. Heat the oven to 400°F/200°C/Gas Mark 6. Roll out the pastry very thinly and cut into six oblongs the same length as your leeks. Roll each leek up in a piece of pastry, seal the joint with water but leave the ends open. Place joint side down on a greased baking tray, brush with beaten egg and bake for 20 minutes until puffed up and golden.

Serve with:

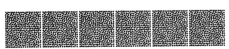 # Tomato Sauce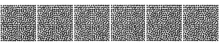

Preparation time: 2 minutes
Cooking time: 10 minutes

Imperial (Metric)

*1 oz (25 g) butter
1 tablespoon flour
1 small onion, finely chopped
1 teaspoon sugar
squeeze lemon juice
½ pint (275 ml) tomato purée
¼ teaspoon dried basil (optional)
salt and black pepper*

American

*2 level tablespoons butter
1 tablespoon flour
1 small onion, finely chopped
1 teaspoon sugar
squeeze lemon juice
1⅓ cups tomato purée
¼ teaspoon dried basil (optional)
salt and black pepper*

1. Melt butter, lightly fry onion over low heat for five minutes.
2. Sprinkle flour over onions and stir, add all other ingredients, stirring until smooth. Test flavour, season with salt and pepper. Serve separately with leek puffs.

Variations (Sauce)

1. A very quick sauce can be made by heating equal quantities of tomato ketchup (catsup) and milk, seasoning with black pepper and sprinkling with finely chopped fresh mint.
2. Mushroom sauce is equally good with this recipe. Substitute ½ lb (225 g) mushrooms for tomato purée and fry them with the onion. Blend with all ingredients and ½ pint (275 ml) (1⅓ cups) stock and reheat before serving.

 # Crudités with Spicy Dip

Preparation time: 20 minutes
Cooking time: nil

This is one of those useful starters which changes according to the vegetables in the garden and always seems to go down well with friends.

Imperial (Metric)

4 oz (110 g) cottage cheese or curd
  cheese
2 tablespoons thick natural yoghurt
2 oz (50 g) roasted peanuts
¼ teaspoon garam masala
¼ teaspoon ground coriander
salt and black pepper
1 clove of garlic, crushed (optional)

American

½ cup Ricotta cheese
2 tablespoons thick natural yoghurt
½ cup roasted peanuts
¼ teaspoon garam masala
¼ teaspoon coriander
salt and black pepper
1 clove of garlic, crushed (optional)

Blend all ingredients and chill for at least an hour. Serve in one large or several small bowls surrounded by thin strips of raw carrot, red and green apple dipped in lemon juice, celery, new French beans, cucumber, stems of Swiss chard and anything else in season such as tiny cauliflower florets.

Variation Avocado Dip
Try this as a change when avocados are cheap. Simply blend the flesh of a large very ripe avocado with a clove of garlic, a squeeze of lemon juice and salt and pepper. This is also delicious served with toast fingers instead of crudités.

 # Baked Onions

Preparation time: 10 minutes
Cooking time: 45 minutes

This is an excellent starter as it is equally delicious hot or cold. For two people you need:

Imperial (Metric)

4 medium onions
2 tablespoons sherry
tablespoon oil
3 tablespoons water
2 tablespoons sesame seeds
2 oz (50 g) small mushrooms

American

4 medium onions
2 tablespoons sherry
tablespoon oil
3 tablespoons water
2 tablespoons sesame seeds
2 oz small mushrooms

(Facing) **Pâtés and Savoury Biscuits:** From back: Mushroom and Vegetable Pâté, Chicken Liver Pâté, Potted Cheese, Mackerel Pâté. At front: Smoked Salmon Pâté. Cheese biscuits — from right: Oatcakes, Cheese Straws, Curry Biscuits, Water Biscuits

1. Preheat oven to 400°F/200°C/Gas Mark 6. Put the whole onions including skins into boiling water and simmer for five minutes. Drain, cool and skin them.
2. Put in an oven proof dish with sherry, water and a sprinkling of salt. Bake for 30 minutes. Meanwhile, heat the oil and fry sesame seeds until golden, then add the sliced mushrooms for two minutes. Scrape the sesame seeds and mushrooms over the onions and return to the oven with foil covering the dish for a further ten minutes. Test the onions to see they are cooked and leave a little longer if necessary.

Salads

Throughout the summer our green salads — which we serve at least four times a week — vary from day to day depending on what is ready, but they usually contain 'Salad Bowl' lettuce, celtuce, 'Little Gem' cos lettuce, land cress, chives, parsley, lovage, the new leaves of dandelions, lemon balm, mint and extras like the first French beans or mangetout when there isn't enough for a vegetable dish.

We make up three varieties of French dressing and keep them in screw top bottles, giving them a good shake before using.

 # Basic Oil and Vinegar (French) Dressing

Preparation time: 2 minutes
Cooking time: nil

Imperial (Metric)

6 tablespoons olive oil or salad oil
1 tablespoon wine vinegar
1 teaspoon mustard powder
1 teaspoon salt (rock salt if possible)
black pepper

American

6 tablespoons olive oil or salad oil
1 tablespoon wine vinegar
1 teaspoon mustard powder
1 teaspoon salt (rock salt if possible)
black pepper

Put everything into a large screw top bottle, shake vigorously until blended. Shake again before using.

Variations
1. Garlic — Put ⅓ of the dressing into another bottle and add a teaspoon of garlic paste or 1 crushed clove.
2. Fines Herbes — Add a teaspoon each of chopped parsley, chopped lovage or chervil and chopped chives to ⅓ basic dressing.
3. Mint — Add 2 teaspoons finely chopped fresh mint to ⅓ basic dressing.

We frequently serve side dishes of potatoes, green beans or tomatoes as salads and find the flavour of freshly gathered vegetables comes through particularly well

(Facing) **Salads:** Clockwise: Rainbow Beans, Chicken Rice Salad, Avocado and Apple Salad, Stuffed Eggs, Prawn and Rice Salad, Tomatoes with Mint Dressing, Yoghurt Dressing

in these dishes. They are very simple to make but the excellence of the ingredients makes them special.

 ## Potato Salad

Simply wash 2 lb (900 g) of small new potatoes and put them in a pan of boiling water with ½ teaspoon salt and a sprig of fresh mint. Simmer for about 25 minutes then drain and tip into salad bowl. Slice or chop them and pour on your chosen dressing while they are still warm. The mint one is perfect and we also like to scatter a little more chopped mint over the dish just before serving.

 ## Green Bean Salad

Boil small runner beans whole or string and slice larger ones first. They need about five or six minutes in salted water. Drain thoroughly, tip into salad bowl and add fines herbes dressing while they are still warm. Before serving, mix in some finely grated lemon peel. Mangetout are also excellent served this way.

 ## Tomato Salad

Thinly slice large tomatoes — we grow 'Marmande' for salads — and spoon a little French dressing on each slice. Add finely chopped basil or a sprinkling of dried basil, and a little black pepper. Mint dressing is also excellent with tomatoes.

If you only have small quantities of new vegetables in the garden and want to stretch them, you'll find that serving them in parsley sauce or a light cheese sauce makes them into a special dish. Young broad beans, broccoli, new potatoes, French beans and whole tiny beets and turnips seem particularly good when served hot this way.

Main Courses

We find marrows particularly useful for main course dishes and before you dismiss them as watery tasteless rings of nothing you might like to try the following recipes which we have enjoyed for years.

 # Marrow Puffs

Preparation time: 15 minutes
Cooking time: 20 minutes, including sauce

Imperial (Metric)

1 medium sized marrow
Flour and water batter (see p. 15)

Parsley Sauce
½ pint (275 ml) milk + ¼ pint
* (150 ml)*
1½ oz (40 g) flour
2 oz (50 g) butter
4 tablespoons chopped parsley
1 teaspoon lemon juice
salt and pepper

American

1 medium sized marrow or squash
Flour and water batter (see p. 15)

Parsley Sauce
1⅓ cups milk + just over ½ cup
3 level tablespoons flour
4 level tablespoons butter
4 tablespoons chopped parsley
1 teaspoon lemon juice
salt and pepper

1. Peel, core and slice marrow. Dip rings into batter and deep fry until puffed up and golden. Drain and keep hot.
2. Make sauce by melting butter in a small pan then adding flour, stirring constantly until smooth. Gradually add milk, beating until smooth. Simmer gently for five minutes stirring from time to time. Beat in the extra ¼ pint of milk, simmer for a minute, season with pepper and salt and add lemon juice just before serving. Hand round separately to pour over marrow puffs.

 # Marrow and Cheese Pie

Preparation time: 15 minutes
Cooking time: 10 minutes plus 30 minutes

Imperial (Metric)

1 medium sized marrow
1 pint (275 ml) milk
8 oz tasty cheese, grated
1 egg
2 oz (50 g) flour
salt and black pepper

American

1 medium sized marrow or squash
1⅓ cups milk
2 cups grated cheese
1 egg
2 heaped tablespoons flour
salt and black pepper

1. Peel, core and slice marrow. If it is very young you can leave the skin on. Place in pan of boiling water and cook for ten minutes. Drain thoroughly and tip into mixing bowl. Mash up with potato masher.

2. Beat together egg, flour, milk and half the cheese. Mix with mashed marrow, season well with salt and black pepper and pour into greased oven proof dish. Sprinkle grated cheese on top and bake at 350°F/180°C/Gas Mark 4 for about 30 minutes until nicely browned.

Variations
1. Replace marrow with 8 good sticks celery.
2. Replace marrow with a large cauliflower or 1 lb (450 g) broccoli spears.
3. Replace marrow with 1 lb (450 g) leeks.

As you can see, variations on this recipe are endless and you will no doubt discover others yourselves.

Desserts

You will find puddings, ice creams, sorbets and desserts using our own fruit in many of the special sections in the book, but we like to serve the first soft fruits quite simply with a sprinkling of sugar and cream or − in the case of blackcurrants and gooseberries − lightly stewed with sugar and served with cream, ice cream or home-made custard. When we get tired of this we start on the variations. It is the same with 'top fruit'. A bowl of freshly picked apples and pears or a dish of ripe plums or grapes cannot be bettered. When we find we have too many to cope with, we give some away and start to freeze and cook the rest.

The great thing about growing for the pot, especially when you have retired, is that once you have got through the hard work like digging − either by taking it slowly or by persuading one of the younger members of the family to help out − you have time to enjoy pottering.

Pottering of course is the only genuinely pleasant aspect of gardening and is best seen as an exercise for two or more people, involving as it does such preliminaries as discussions about the weather, a survey of the property, however small, to ascertain how each crop is doing and further discussions as to whether the harvest looks like being better or worse than in previous years.

It is then usually time for a relaxing cup of tea before proceeding to such tasks as watering, removing any giant size weeds that are actually interfering with the growth of their edible counterparts and, of course, picking whatever produce is ready.

By this time you will have forgotten any of the hard work you may have had to do, any money you may have had to spend on seeds and fertilisers and the whole thing will seem like the nearest you can get to a free lunch. Indeed it probably would be just that, except for the fact that for people who have the time − and that means retired people − nature has provided quite a few things that come even cheaper than your own garden produce and all you need to know in order to take advantage of this bounty is what to look for and where to look.

5

Something for Nothing

They do say there's no such thing as a free lunch but in fact there are lots of free lunches and dinners around that cost nothing much more than the effort required to reach out for them. And that, if you are retired, is the equivalent of a gold deckled invitation.

Accept the invitation and you'll find that, now you have the time to look around, the world is full of good things to eat which are largely neglected simply because they are hanging on trees and bushes instead of being neatly packaged on supermarket shelves.

Of course, a lot depends on where you live but, looking out of our front window and across a busy road about a mile from the centre of the city, I can see on the river bank the ingredients for half-a-dozen different sorts of jams, desserts, teas and wines and the strange thing is, that unless we take the trouble to pick them, they will almost certainly be wasted.

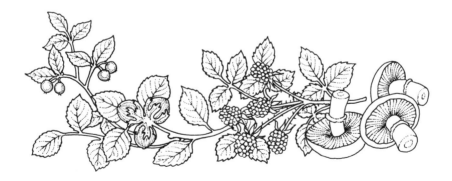

Blackberries

Out in the country things are different but even there it is largely the older folk who remember the hard times and keep alive the foraging tradition of the real countrymen. They even have their own time honoured foraging grounds, as we found whem we went blackberrying for the first time on our very own fields.

We had just bought an old farm house and a few acres of land and found to our delight that the hedgerows which paralleled some of dry stone walls were heavy with blackberries. Thanks to the almost constant rain they were splendidly sweet and juicy and, as they looked like being one of the few crops we would get that year, we set off with our baskets for the nearest field.

We'd been picking for about ten minutes and congratulating ourselves on having found such a good spot when we heard shouting and turned round to find an irate elderly villager bearing down on us, brandishing a nasty looking knobbly walking stick.

As 'comers-in' there didn't seem to be much point in arguing with custom and usage so we beat a hasty retreat and, though we subsequently became good friends with the old chap who taught us townies quite a bit about the countryside, there was always a tacit agreement that those particular bushes were 'his'.

Mind you, when you consider that blackberries make a good dessert if you merely wash them, sprinkle them with sugar and pour on a little thin cream or the cream from the top of the milk, you can appreciate that they are a valuable commodity.

Of course that's just for starters, as the blackberries that are just waiting to be picked up in the course of a gentle stroll are one of the most versatile fruits. Even before you start to think of cooking them you could, for example, shove them through a blender with some sugar and a drop of water, then sieve and drink straightaway or pour over ice cream or mix with milk for a marvellously refreshing milk-shake.

Blackberry wine is a favourite among country wines and you could also make a blackberry cordial – one of Molly's mother's favourites – to keep for use against colds in the winter.

Blackberry and apple pie comes high on my list and, if you make a couple to eat and a couple to put in the freezer, you'll have a splendid memento of your late summer blackberrying expedition; although in addition to the pies, of course you could have other reminders like blackberry jelly, blackberry and apple jam and blackberry sorbet.

Just thinking about blackberry sorbet is enough to make my mouth water, especially when I know that one fruit alone is going to save us pounds and that as yet we have hardly begun to examine the freebies nature has to offer to those of use who have the time to look for them.

It is worth remembering that Man was once a hunter gatherer and that setting out for a stroll armed with a length of stick and a basket is a lot closer to our natural condition than popping round to the supermarket. It is also a great deal cheaper.

Talking of baskets, it is a good idea to take a pair of gardening gloves, a walking stick with a handle and several plastic bags with closures along with you whenever you are out on a foraging expedition, the latter because in addition to holding fruits and so on they come in useful if someone presents you with a few cuttings.

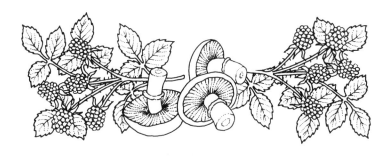

 # Blackberry Wine

Ready to drink in 6 months to a year

Imperial (Metric)

4 lb (1.8 kg) blackberries
3 lb (1.35 kg) granulated sugar
1 gallon (4.5 litres) water
wine yeast

American

4 lb blackberries
6 cups granulated sugar
10 pints water
wine yeast

1. Wash fruit very well. Crush in large crock or bucket. Pour over all the boiling water.
2. Mix yeast according to instructions on packet and add when the fruit has cooled.
3. Strain through nylon sieve into sugar. Stir to dissolve sugar then pour into a fermentation jar or demi-john up to shoulder and fit airlock. Keep spare juice in another jar also with airlock.
4. When fermentation stops foaming up, top up with spare juice and refit airlock. Leave until it clears then rack off* with syphon from sediment into clean jar. Refit airlock.
5. Allow to clear again for three months and rack off again.

Bottle when fermentation has ceased. Ready in a year but try a drop in six months.

 # Blackberry and Apple Jam

Preparation time: 10 minutes
Cooking time: about 20 minutes

Imperial (Metric)

1 lb (450 g) blackberries
1 lb (450 g) cooking apples
   (after peeling and coring)
2 lb granulated sugar
2 tablespoons water

American

1 lb blackberries
1 lb cooking apples (after peeling and
   coring)
4 cups granulated sugar
2 tablespoons water

1. Chop apples, simmer in water until tender, then add well washed berries, simmer for 10 minutes.
2. Stir in sugar until dissolved then boil fast for 10 minutes till set, constantly stirring. Test in a little cold water on a saucer.

---

* Racking off: Remove the cork and airlock and use a 3 ft (1 metre) length of thin clear plastic tubing to siphon off the clear wine into a second demi-john. Suck at it gently to get it started and place the second jar at a lower level than the full one. Take care not to disturb the sediment — replace cork and airlock and leave to clear.

 Blackberry Jelly

Preparation time: 2 minutes
Cooking time: 45 minutes

Imperial (Metric)

2 lb (450 g) blackberries
juice of 2 lemons
4 tablespoons water
2 lb (900 g) granulated sugar

American

2 lb blackberries
juice of 2 lemons
4 tablespoons water
4 cups granulated sugar

1. Wash the blackberries thoroughly and place in a heavy saucepan with the water. Stew gently with the lid on for 20 minutes.
2. Mash up with potato masher to release juice, add the sugar and lemon and stir to dissolve the sugar completely. Takes about 15 minutes.
3. Turn up heat and boil rapidly for ten minutes, stirring to prevent sticking. Heat a large baking bowl and a couple of jam jars. Place a fine sieve lined with gauze over the bowl and press the blackberry jelly through into the basin. Fill the jars quickly, cover with waxed paper and fasten down when cool. If the jelly starts to set before you get it into the jars just reheat it slightly.

This only keeps for a month, but we've never known it last so long.

 Blackberry Sorbet

Preparation time: 20 minutes spread over 3 hours
Cooking time: 5 minutes

Imperial (Metric)

1 lb (450 g) blackberries
4 oz (110 g) granulated sugar
5 fluid oz (150 ml) water
2 tablespoons rose water

American

1 lb blackberries
1/2 cup granulated sugar
just over 1/2 cup water
2 tablespoons rose water

1. Simmer sugar and water for five minutes. Leave to cool.
2. Wash blackberries thoroughly and rub through a sieve into a bowl. Add sugar syrup and rose water to the fruit purée. Stir well.
3. Spoon into plastic containers and freeze for an hour. Remove from freezer and stir.
4. Leave in freezer two hours. Tip out of containers, scraping round sides and whisk until smooth and fluffy. Pour back into containers and freeze at least overnight. Serve decorated with sprigs of mint.

I've mentioned blackberries first because, while everyone knows what a blackberry looks like and you can find them in almost every hedgerow, some of the other free lunches are less familiar, while others aren't easily recognised as food at all. The fact is that there is so much free food lying around that survival specialists, like people from the SAS and similar organizations, can live off the land in most parts of the world for days, if not weeks.

Elderflowers

Between a simple blackberrying expedition and a survival exercise there's a whole range of tastes and expertise and it's really up to the individual to decide what sorts of free food are for them. In our case, for example, we already find that we have time to collect and process most of the familiar fruits of the countryside and our horizons are gradually expanding to take in things like leaf teas and the less well known fungi.

For instance, we are absolutely sold on the elder tree which grows in profusion in most parts of the city, never mind the countryside, because both the flowers and the fruit have a myriad uses. We use the flowers to make elderflower champagne and to cook elderflower fritters and the berries to make a very palatable red wine. They also make good jam and jelly and you can even dry them to use like currants.

 # Elderflower Champagne

Ready to drink in two months

Imperial (Metric)

6 large heads of elderflowers
2 lb (900 g) granulated sugar
2 tablespoons white vinegar
2 large lemons
1 gallon (4.5 litres) water

American

6 large heads of elderflowers
4 cups granulated sugar
2 tablespoons white vinegar
2 large lemons
10 pints water

1. Shake the elderflowers to remove any dust or insects. Place in large container, i.e. crock or plastic bucket. Add the lemons cut in thin slices, the cold water and the vinegar and stir in the sugar. Cover with a cloth and leave to stand for 24 hours. Stir again.

2. Strain off carefully and pour liquid into strong screw top bottles. Leave for two months before drinking, but release and retighten screw tops every third day to release excess fizz or the bottles may burst.

This is so light, sparking and refreshing that we never make enough of it and always vow to fill the cellar with it next year.

 # Elderflower Fritters

Preparation time: 20 minutes
Cooking time: 5 minutes each batch

Like lettuce fritters, this is one of those recipes that sounds a bit ridiculous until you actually taste.

Imperial (Metric)

12 heads elderflowers
2 eggs
1 pint (570 ml) milk
pinch salt
1 teaspoon melted butter
4 oz (110 g) flour
1 lemon
cooking oil

American

12 heads elderflowers
2 eggs
2½ cups milk
pinch salt
1 teaspoon melted butter
1 cup flour
1 lemon
cooking oil

1. Remove flower stalks, leaving flower clusters intact. Wash in cold water very gently so as not to break flowerets. Shake gently.
2. Make smooth batter with eggs, milk, flour, butter and salt.
3. Dip flower clusters carefully in batter and deep fry in hot oil for a few minutes until golden brown. Drain well and keep hot until all are done. Serve sprinkled with sugar and with lemon quarters.

There are at least 70 edible wild plants to be found in most parts of the United Kingdom — the figures are the same or better for many other countries — but to recognize them involves either careful study or a bit of friendly on the spot tuition and by and large tuition is better. After all, it's not a lot of use knowing that the bulb of the common Star of Bethlehem can be peeled and used as a boiled vegetable if you don't happen to live near the rough grasslands of East Anglia where *Ornithogalum umbellatum* is mainly to be found. On the other hand, if you are within striking distance of East Anglia, a visit to a village pub might yield useful intelligence as to the whereabouts and appearance of the plant as well as a few traditional recipes featuring its use.

This sort of local knowledge is invaluable when it comes to edible wild plants but it might be as well to wait until a second or third visit before asking leading questions, as you might otherwise find yourself the victim of a local prankster.

Take a notebook with you on all foraging expeditions to write down not only anything you may glean from the locals — a notebook can give you the look of a serious researcher — but to note down for future reference the location of particularly productive sites.

Dandelions and Nettles

While you are building up your list of free edibles, and of course testing them out to see if you like them, you can continue to forage for the sort of things even I can recognise, like dandelions. Use the young leaves in salads or braise them as a vegetable. You can blanch the leaves like chicory by putting a pot over the plant or a couple of wedged stones, although we use the leaves green. You can use the roots for a vegetable too if you give them a good scrub, cut them into thin strips and braise in stock until they are tender. No wonder the French have elevated this humble weed to an honorary vegetable and can't understand why our gardeners destroy it.

Another unlikely contender in this category is the nettle, the tops of which make a splendid soup and a handful of ground elder — that invasive weed — is very tasty in soups instead of the more usual cabbage or spinach. Or you can try a nettle omelette.

 Nettle Omelette

Simmer the tops of young shoots in a little stock for a few minutes then chop and mix with a spoonful of grated cheese, season well and use to fill omelette. If you have only one egg, make up a batch of pancakes and use this as a filling.

 Nettle and Dandelion Beer

Cooking time: 1 hour
Waiting time: three days

Imperial (Metric)	American
2 good handfuls of young nettles	*2 good handfuls of young nettles*
2 good handfuls dandelion leaves and a few roots	*2 good handfuls dandelion leaves and a few roots*
2 medium sticks rhubarb	*2 medium sticks rhubarb*
1½ lb (700 g) demerara sugar	*3 cups soft brown sugar*
1 gallon (4.5 litres) water	*10 pints water*
1 lemon, thinly sliced	*1 lemon, thinly sliced*
1 teaspoon ground ginger	*1 teaspoon ground ginger*
½ oz (10 g) brewer's yeast	*1 tablespoon brewer's yeast*

1. Put all ingredients, except yeast, in a large pan, bring to the boil and simmer for an hour. Strain and leave to cool.
2. When liquid is lukewarm, mix a little with yeast and stir it well. Pour into large container — crock or plastic bucket — and leave covered for 12 hours. Bottle in strong screw top bottles. You can drink this in three days and it will keep for about a fortnight.

Variation
Substitute burdock leaves for nettles to make Dandelion and Burdock Beer.

Leaves

Incidentally, one minor disadvantage of being at home more than before you retired is that you tend to drink more tea which, although pleasant enough, does tend to be expensive. With this in mind it is definitely worth experimenting with herb and flower teas which can be had for free.

Using the ubiquitous elder for example, you merely infuse a head of fresh flowers or two teaspoons of dried ones in a pint of boiling water and leave for two minutes before straining. Serve with lemon and sugar or honey. Burnet leaves and lemon balm leaves can be dried and crumbled and used just like ordinary tea. A great many of the herbal and flower teas were around long before Indian and China tea became popular and a lot of them have useful medical properties, especially as an aid to digestion or to relieve headache.

Other edible leaves come from trees such as hawthorn and beech, the young leaves of which can be used as salad or as a green vegetable.

Roots

There are roots like wild salsify which are excellent when peeled and soaked in cold water with a drop of lemon juice before boiling them until tender enough to eat with butter. This is also the way to cook the cultivated sort which is easy to grow.

Then there are roots which can be made into a kind of flour and others which can provide a thickening for stews or, like the Sea Holly, can be made into sweetmeats, while the French used to roast the roots of dandelions during the war to make a coffee substitute. In fact pursuing the more esoteric edible plants could be a very worthwhile money-saving hobby, but you could make a start with the more common varieties we have mentioned.

Apart from laver bread, which we weren't all that keen on, we haven't tried much seaweed although there are at least four other edible types including kelp, which can be used as a salad ingredient, dulse which can be fried and carragheen moss which can be made into a vegetable gelatine for use in either sweet or savoury dishes.

Fortunately we are on safer ground when it comes to herbs and spices because we use quite a lot of them, some of which are cultivated, some of which like borage and lemon balm just happened to drop by our garden as they were passing, and others which we gather from the hedgerows.

Fungi

It's a pity that there isn't another and more pleasing name for these delicious items of free food, but perhaps the rather off-putting sound is worthwhile if it makes people take care. Having said that, there are not all that many deadly fungi − in the United Kingdom at any rate − and there are a hundred superb tasting, harmless varieties that are absolutely free.

The best thing to do is to get hold of a first class illustrated guide and to combine this wherever possible with local knowledge, bearing in mind the fact that the fungus has to be large enough, when you pick it, to be compared with its picture.

The common or horse mushroom is perhaps the easiest to find and if you are lucky enough a handful of them gathered on an early morning walk can turn an egg and a bit of bacon into a feast. In a field near my sister's house in Scotland you can find mushrooms some years as big as dinner plates and fatter than a good steak. They are absolutely marvellous — but you have to get up early to beat the village kids to them, especially as they seem to know in advance where they are going to spring up and regard them as their pocket money because they sell them to local shops.

Next easiest to identify are the chanterelles and the morel which has a cap like a honeycomb. We find the best way of coping with fungi is to add one more to our list of known edible and enjoyable ones every now and again. This may not be very courageous but as, unlike the French who have official fungi inspectors to check their haul for dicey specimens, we have only our own experience to go on, it does seem the safest way.

Incidentally, while you have a perfect right to forage hedgerows, commons and woodland for fungi, nuts and most other edible plants, it is courteous to ask the farmer if it's okay to go on his land and your good manners could even save you an unexpected encounter with a bull. Don't forget, however, that you must not dig up any plants.

In our part of the world there are so many canals, river banks, footpaths, woods and abandoned railway lines, not to mention hedgerows, that it is rarely necessary to go onto agricultural land for things like blackberries.

 # Mushroom and Hazelnut Pâté

Preparation time: 15 minutes
Cooking time: 10 minutes

Imperial (Metric)	**American**
4 oz (110 g) hazelnuts	*1 cup hazelnuts*
4 oz (110 g) mushrooms, chopped	*1 cup mushrooms, chopped*
½ small onion, chopped fine	*½ small onion, chopped fine*
2 tablespoons soft breadcrumbs	*2 tablespoons soft breadcrumbs*
clove of garlic, crushed	*clove of garlic, crushed*
level tablespoon butter	*level tablespoon butter*
salt and black pepper	*salt and black pepper*
juice and grated rind of 1 lemon	*juice and grated rind of 1 lemon*

1. Grind nuts to fine powder.
2. Cook onion and chopped mushrooms very gently in butter.
3. Put all ingredients in blender and whizz until smooth. If the pâté seems dry, add a little more melted butter. Chill before serving.

This freezes well so we usually make enough for several small pots. Chopped chives, parsley or the leaves of lovage or celery can be used to garnish. The pâté is excellent on toast or with the small sesame crackers (see p. 162).

Stuffed Mushrooms

Preparation time: 10 minutes
Cooking time: 30 minutes

For this recipe you need the giant flat mushrooms.

Imperial (Metric)

5 large mushrooms
4 oz (110 g) fresh breadcrumbs
level tablespoon melted butter
juice and grated rind of 1 lemon
crushed clove of garlic or 2 teaspoons
*   garlic paste*
salt and black pepper

American

5 large mushrooms
1 cup fresh breadcrumbs
level tablespoon melted butter
juice and grated rind of 1 lemon
crushed clove of garlic or 2 teaspoons
*   garlic paste*
salt and black pepper

1. Finely chop one mushroom and stalks of others, mix in bowl with all ingredients except 4 remaining mushrooms.
2. Put 4 mushrooms on a large greased oven dish, press stuffing mixture into each cap, cover with foil and bake in oven 375°F/190°C/Gas Mark 5 for 30 minutes.

This serves two for a main course or four for a first course.

Berries and Rosehips

In the North of England we used to find loads of bilberries — also known as blueberries, whortleberries, hurts and worts — which make splendid pies and tarts. Wild cherries, crab apples and sloes can often be found and there are supposed to be wild raspberries although I can't remember ever coming across any.

Easier to find and to recognise are the wonderful rosehips which make great jam and a marvellous syrup which is full of vitamins as well as being good for tickly throats.

Here again you might do well to go for the easy fruits first and gradually widen the scope of your foraging, because there really is plenty to go at before you start on the esoteric stuff.

 # Rosehip Jam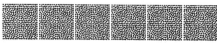

This is one of the easiest jams to make and you have the pleasure of knowing that you are making something special as it is not usually obtainable in the shops.

Preparation time: 5 minutes
Cooking time: about 1 hour

Imperial (Metric)

1 lb (450 g) rosehips
½ pint (275 ml) water
granulated sugar as below

American

2 cups rosehips
1⅓ cups water
granulated sugar as below

1. Simmer rosehips until tender — this depends on size and variety. Liquidise and sieve.
2. Put in pan with sugar equal in weight to sieved pulp. Simmer till thick. Pot and cover.

 # Rosehip Jelly

Preparation time: 15 minutes
Cooking time: about 1 hour plus time for straining

The cooking time again depends on the size and variety of the hips.

Imperial (Metric)

1 lb (450 g) rosehips
2 lbs (900 g) apples
1 pint (570 ml) water
granulated sugar as below
juice of 1 lemon

American

2 cups rosehips
2 lbs apples
2½ cups water
granulated sugar as below
juice of 1 lemon

1. Chop apples and simmer in half of water until pulped; strain through jelly bag or large nylon sieve lined with a piece of chemist's gauze.
2. Simmer rosehips with rest of water until soft. Strain through jelly bag. Combine juice of both and put in pan with juice of lemon and equal weight of sugar, stirring till sugar is dissolved.
3. Boil to a fast set. Test in cold water, pot and cover.

 # Rose Petal Jam

Cooking time: about 30 minutes
Resting time: overnight

Molly's mother used to make this to serve with home-made scones and always insisted that wild roses were best.

Imperial (Metric)	**American**
4 oz (110 g) rose petals	*1 cup of rose petals*
1½ lbs (700 g) granulated sugar	*3 cups granulated sugar*
1 tablespoon lemon juice	*1 tablespoon lemon juice*
¼ pint (150 ml) rosewater	*just over ½ cup rosewater*

1. Put the rose petals in a large baking bowl; bring water, sugar, lemon juice and rosewater to the boil and simmer for five minutes.
2. Pour over petals, cover with cloth and leave overnight.
3. Next day pour the mixture into a large pan, simmer very gently stirring continuously until the syrup thickens. This takes about 30 minutes. Pot and cover.

Rose petals can also be used to make an unusual flavoured vinegar which gives a pleasant tang to dressings for summer salads. You simply fill a wide mouthed glass jar with rose petals, cover with white vinegar, cork or seal and leave on a sunny window ledge for two weeks. Strain before using.

Fish

If you live within easy reach of a lake or the seaside — and in England the sea is never more than 70 miles away — the water is a cornucopia of free food, especially if you enjoy fishing as a sport. Of course people may get a little upset if they find you chucking a bent pin into their exclusive stretch of salmon river but there is plenty of free water around for the taking of less aristocratic fish.

I'm not a fisherman but I have been very successful in fishing from Scottish piers and, even more so, from a rowing boat off Tynemouth where, thanks to local knowledge, I was able to position the boat over what trawlermen call a 'fish shop'. This was a place where the fish were so plentiful that you didn't really need bait and in a few minutes the bottom of the boat was usually filled with giant codling, so many that my landlady was unable to use them all and I was forced to give them away.

Then one day as I was walking past the hotel at the end of the road the under manager asked me if I had any fish to spare, with the result that for much of my stay in the North East of England I drank free — which means that people who catch fish in retirement to cook in retirement might swap their surplus for a bottle of wine to go with it.

Incidentally, it is essential to get a weather forecast before venturing even a short distance from the shore, no matter what the weather may look like — and to

(Facing) **Summer Ices and Puddings:** Centre: Apple Jelly. Clockwise: Cassata with Chocolate Orange Juice and Walnuts, Strawberry Mousse, Poor Parson's Water Ice, Summer Pudding, Raspberry Ice Cream with Fruit

let someone on shore know where you are going. It is also a good idea to go out with a local the first two or three times as well as taking all the normal precautions like wearing the right gear.

A lot safer — though here again one has to be careful of the tide and the weather — is fishing from the beach, but this can be less than cost effective in terms of effort and you could do better with a long line with a hundred or so hooks which you put out at night and pull in again in the morning. Find out what the local form is; as a general rule nobody will object to your taking enough fish for yourself and a few to swap but if you take more you could, as the Chinese say, be breaking somebody's rice bowl which is no way to make friends.

One of the finest sources of free food is the sea shore where there is lots of fine fare to be had just for the picking and digging. Most shellfish make good eating and the things to remember are to keep well away from sewage outlets and to eat shellfish only in the months with an 'R' in them. This 'R' rule isn't hard and fast but it is an easy one to remember and shellfish are best collected when the weather is reasonably cold.

Make sure any mussels are firmly closed, get rid of any that aren't and scrub the remainder before cooking.

Shrimps and prawns are easy to find in rock pools on many parts of the coast — just make sure that the water is clean where you find them and cook them until they turn pink. You can eat the shrimps as they are but it is best to peel the prawns and use the shells to boost your fish stock.

Often it is stupid prejudice which stops people taking full advantage of the free gifts that nature has to offer. For example, our garden is full of perfectly good huge snails which we have never thought of eating even though we sometimes have to kill them if we don't want to lose all our crops.

The silly thing is that although we know that they are excellent eating and they are feeding on nothing but the best in our garden we still hesitate, even though in France we have enjoyed escargots. It seems even sillier now that a friend of ours has begun farming snails about half an hour's drive from our home for export to France and Japan!

However it does help to make the point that it's no use eating free food if you don't fancy it — after all there are bound to be plenty of items amongst nature's giveaways that you will be able to eat with pleasure. And now that you've retired, you have the time to look for them and to prepare them to your taste.

(Facing) **Dorothy's Baking Day:** Dorothy's Bread, Rolls, Egg Custard Tart, Gooseberry and Apple Pie. Left: Easiest Bread in the World

6

Fast Food

Cooking in retirement is all about pleasing yourself and taking things easy; so if you feel like buying a packet of fish fingers there's no need to feel guilty about it. After all, served up with fresh garden peas, new potatoes and some home-made parsley sauce they can be delicious.

As far as we are concerned I have to confess that we too have been known to buy the odd item of convenience food.

Of course there's convenience food and convenience food, some execrable, some pretty good, some exceedingly dear and some so reasonable you wonder how the makers can do it at the price. Unfortunately, makers of convenience foods — like the manufacturers of everything else — are in business to make profits, so unless they have passed on the benefits of scale you are liable to find yourself paying over the odds for most of their products while, at the same time, much of their food is made for the average consumer which you, as someone with a lively interest in cooking, cannot be.

Even so, whatever the professional gourmets may say, convenience foods are no more immoral or against natural law than mass production cars; it's just that in both cases you have to be particular about what you buy and it's sometimes advisable to add a few extras.

Check the price of the equivalent fresh items against the price of what is in the packet or tin and have a good look to see exactly what you are buying. Don't just read the name of the item, which may suggest what the manufacturers wish you to believe is in the packet; read the small print list of ingredients which will tell you, for example, if Thingummybob's 'Lobsterbits' are indeed lobster or made of cod, cochineal and Lord knows what else.

Given a reasonable fast food item from the shops you can always make it into a tastier dish with the addition of something of your own, even if it is only a drop of home-made sauce, or even packet sauce with a spoonful of chopped fresh herbs.

If you have a deep freeze don't forget that, apart from a few items, it's almost always better and cheaper to have some fast food of your own ready and waiting. Exceptions are baby onions in white sauce which are so fiddly to do that we always keep a packet in the freezer and frozen puff pastry which is so excellent we only make our own when we are doing a large batch of baking.

As we mentioned in a previous chapter, if you have a microwave oven this could answer most of your fast food requirements, providing you have a well stocked cupboard and freezer.

Assuming you have a deep freeze a good idea is to make both savoury and sweet pies in small foil dishes or even patty tins, a dozen at a time. Wrap them individually, then put in a labelled plastic bag or box so that you don't need to defrost and cook a large pie when you want a quick meal. Molly's Auntie Nell came up with this idea — she always makes up batches of Uncle Frank's favourite meat pies and apple pies for him to heat up when she visits her sister. You'll find her recipes below.

Fast Food from the Freezer

It is always useful to have plenty of bread and spreads of some sort in small containers in the freezer because then at least you won't starve and, while you're tucking into hot rolls and pâté, you can take your time drinking a nice of cup of tea and thinking about what else is available.

Of course if you have planned things correctly you should be sitting in the sun or in front of the fire with your feet up because you will have prepared a list of meals and dishes — cooked on an energetic day for just such an occasion — together with a note about where to find them in the freezer. This is where your list on the side of the freezer or on the wall nearby is invaluable. If you list everything as you put it in the freezer and cross it off as you use it, you'll have a good guide to shopping and to your available stores. It's a bit of a chore marking things up each time — especially if you are not an organised person — but you soon get into the habit. Here are some of the fast food items you might like to have on your freezer list.

 Auntie Nell's Individual Meat Pies

Preparation time: 20 minutes
Cooking time: total 40 minutes

Pastry

Imperial (Metric)

6 oz (175 g) self-raising flour
3 oz (75 g) lard or half lard/half margarine
¼ teaspoon salt
3 tablespoons water

American

1½ cups self-rising flour
just under ½ cup lard or half lard/half margarine
¼ teaspoon salt
3 tablespoons water

1. Mix flour and salt, rub in fat and mix to a soft dough with water.
2. Divide into eight pieces.

Filling

Imperial (Metric)	American
8 oz (225 g) minced beef	*1 cup ground beef*
1 small onion, chopped	*1 small onion, chopped*
1 teaspoon gravy granules	*1 teaspoon gravy granules*
1 beef cube	*1 beef cube*
¼ teaspoon salt	*¼ teaspoon salt*
½ pint (150 ml) water	*just over 1 cup water*

1. Put all in a pan, bring to boil and simmer for ten minutes. Allow to cool and remove fat from surface.
2. Grease 4 foil pie dishes (4 inches (10 cm) if deep, 5 inches (13 cm) if shallow).
3. Line with rolled out pastry, fill with meat mixture and season with pepper and pinch of herbs if liked. Damp edges and cover with pastry. Press down edges with fork.
4. Brush tops with milk and bake on middle shelf (425°F/220°C/Gas Mark 7) for 25 minutes.

Variations

1. Apple — Peel 1½ lb (700 g) apples, slice them and put in a pan with 1 tablespoon water, squeeze lemon juice and 4 oz (110 g) (½ cup) sugar. Cook until soft, then continue as for meat pies.
2. Cheese and Onion — Peel and chop 1½ lb (700 g) onions. Boil in a little water until soft. Drain and divide between pastry bases. Add salt and pepper and tablespoon grated cheese to each pie. Cover with pastry and continue as for meat pies.

Wrap these separately to keep in freezer. They cook from frozen and are improved by brushing tops with milk before cooking.

 Fish Cakes

Preparation time: 30 minutes

Cooking time: 10 minutes each batch

Imperial (Metric)	American
1 lb (450 g) can tuna or pink salmon	*1 lb can tuna or pink salmon*
1 lb (450 g) potatoes	*1 lb potatoes*
salt, pepper	*salt, pepper*
tablespoon tomato ketchup	*tablespoon catsup*
2 eggs	*2 eggs*
breadcrumbs	*breadcrumbs*
1 tablespoon chopped parsley	*1 tablespoon chopped parsley*
vegetable oil for frying	*vegetable oil for frying*
little flour	*little flour*

1. Drain and flake fish, removing any bones. Peel and boil potatoes. Drain and press through sieve.

2. Place potatoes in bowl with fish, seasonings and 1 beaten egg. Mix thoroughly.

3. Beat up second egg in small bowl. Turn fish mixture onto floured board and shape into a thick roll, adding a little flour if necessary. Place in refrigerator to firm up. Divide into 12 pieces, shape into flat cakes, dip in beaten egg then place on a plate of breadcrumbs.

Cover with more dry breadcrumbs until evenly coated. Freeze unwrapped on a tray then put in polythene bags two at a time to store in freezer.

To serve, heat up a little oil, add the frozen fish cakes and fry on each side gently for about five minutes until cooked through and well browned.

Variations

1. Replace fish by grated onion and ¾ lb (350 g) (3 cups) grated cheese. Cook from frozen.

2. Replace fish by grated onion and ¾ lb (350 g) (3 cups) sliced mushrooms. Cook from frozen.

3. Replace fish by 1 grated onion and ¾ lb (350 g) (2 cups) chopped cooked meat — corned beef, roast beef, roast ham, etc., and teaspoonful Worcestershire Sauce. Thaw these at room temperature for 1½ hours before cooking.

Pâtés

Molly's father always used to take over the cooking during summer camping or caravanning holidays and became even more interested in trying out new recipes when he retired. Here are some of his favourite pâtés. None takes longer than 15 minutes to make.

 # Avocado Pâté (For four people)

Preparation time: 5 minutes

Cooking time: nil

Imperial (Metric)

2 large ripe avocados
12 green olives
1 clove garlic, crushed
2 teaspoons lemon juice
salt and black pepper

American

2 large ripe avocados
12 green olives
1 clove garlic, crushed
2 teaspoons lemon juice
salt and black pepper

Scoop out the flesh of the avocados and blend with olives, garlic and seasoning until creamy. Chill for at least one hour.

 # Cheese Pâté

Preparation time: 10 minutes
Cooking time: nil

Imperial (Metric)

4 oz (110 g) hard cheese, grated
2 oz (50 g) melted butter or margarine
2 tablespoons dry cider
1 teaspoon dry mustard
black pepper
½ teaspoon Worcestershire Sauce
heaped tablespoon chopped chives

American

1 cup grated hard cheese
4 tablespoons melted butter or
  margarine
2 tablespoons dry cider
1 teaspoon dry mustard
black pepper
½ teaspoon Worcestershire Sauce
heaped tablespoon chopped chives

1. Simply mix everything thoroughly and press into attractive pots.
2. Refrigerate until cold.

Variations
Replace chives with chopped fresh mint, or chopped parsley and lemon balm. This freezes well in small lidded plastic containers.

 # Smoked Mackerel Pâté

Preparation time: 15 minutes
Cooking time: nil

Imperial (Metric)

Medium smoked mackerel weighing
  about 4 oz (110 g)
juice and grated rind of small lemon
3 oz (75 g) curd cheese
1 oz (25 g) melted butter
black pepper
tablespoon chopped parsley
pinch nutmeg

American

Medium smoked mackerel weighing
  about 4 oz
juice and grated rind of small lemon
just under ½ cup curd or Ricotta
  cheese
2 tablespoons melted butter
black pepper
tablespoon chopped parsley
pinch nutmeg

1. Skin and flake fish and either mash up all ingredients or whizz in blender.
2. Put into small pots and refrigerate. Serve with brown bread and a watercress salad.

Variations
1. Replace mackerel with smoked salmon bits and omit nutmeg.
2. Replace mackerel with smoked haddock or kipper.

These fish pâtés can be made with frozen fish but are best eaten the same day, so unless you are inundated with guests it is best to make them in small quantities.

Chicken Liver Pâté

Preparation time: 10 minutes
Cooking time: 6 minutes

Imperial (Metric)	American
8 oz (225 g) chicken livers	*8 oz chicken livers*
1 small onion	*1 small onion*
1 teaspoon (5 ml) dried mustard	*1 teaspoon dried mustard*
1 teaspoon (5 ml) dried oregano	*1 teaspoon dried oregano*
salt and pepper	*salt and pepper*
4 teaspoons (20 ml) brandy	*4 teaspoons brandy*
5 oz (150 g) butter	*just over ½ cup butter*
1 teaspoon minced garlic (optional)	*1 teaspoon minced garlic (optional)*

1. Lightly sauté finely chopped onion, garlic and chicken livers for 6 minutes in 1 oz (25 g) (2 tablespoons) butter.
2. Melt remaining butter and put all ingredients including chicken liver mixture into blender. Whizz for 30 seconds.
3. Press into earthenware pots. If liked, decorate top with thin slices of lemon and cover with a thin film of melted butter. Refrigerate at least overnight.

Nut Pâté

Preparation time: 15 minutes
Cooking time: nil

Imperial (Metric)	American
4 oz (110 g) roasted peanuts	*1 cup roasted peanuts*
4 oz (110 g) cream cheese	*½ cup cream cheese*
1 clove garlic or 1 small onion, finely chopped	*1 clove garlic or 1 small onion, chopped finely*
1 tablespoon fresh parsley, chopped	*1 tablespoon fresh parsley, chopped*
black pepper	*black pepper*
few drops of Tabasco	*few drops of Tabasco*

Grind nuts, crush garlic and blend all ingredients. If a crunchier pâté is preferred, grind half of nuts only and chop the other half. Add the chopped nuts after blending. Spoon into pottery dishes and serve with brown bread or melba toast.

 # Melba Toast

Very lightly toast both sides of slices of bread. Carefully cut through each slice using a serrated knife and place cut side up under the grill on moderate heat. The toast will curl up. Serve on a napkin in a bread basket. This is very attractive with pâtés or a parsley and lemon butter.

Soups, of course, are ideal freezer standbys for days when you don't feel like cooking but so are small containers of savoury mushrooms — either plain sautéed mushrooms or a mixture of mushroom and chopped onion lightly fried. These can be quickly heated from frozen for a tasty meal on toast.

Desserts

Plain vanilla ice cream is a marvellous basis for quick desserts as well as more elaborate ones. You'll find a recipe for the home-made variety in the section on ice-creams and sorbets, although there are several good commercial varieties. Try to keep a large container always in the freezer and make up some fruit sauces to go with it.

 # Pineapple Fruit Sauce

Preparation time: 5 minutes
Cooking time: nil

Imperial (Metric)

1 large (13 oz) (375 g) can pineapple
2 level tablespoons caster sugar
grated rind and juice of 1 lemon
2 tablespoons sherry

American

1 large 13 oz can pineapple
2 level tablespoons caster sugar
grated rind and juice of 1 lemon
2 tablespoons sherry

Blend all ingredients, including juice from can of fruit, pour into small containers and freeze.

When required either allow to defrost at room temperature or heat very gently in a saucepan. Pour over a plain sponge or serve with ice cream.

Variations
Substitute apricots or peaches (tinned or fresh) or tinned oranges for pineapple.

It is a good idea to put any small quantities of left-over stewed fruit into small foil containers or plastic bags in the freezer. Even a very small amount with a crumble topping of brown sugar and breadcrumbs or crushed biscuit and sugar popped under the grill (broiler) for a few minutes makes a much more satisfying pudding than just a spoonful of fruit. If you haven't a freezer, there are lots of quick dishes you can make from your store cupboard.

 # Fruit Whip

Another idea for any small quantity of tinned or cooked soft fruit is to blend the fruit for a few seconds then mix it with cream and spoon into a tall glass. Add a spoonful of sherry if you really want to spoil yourself.

Fritters

One of the quickest and most satisfying meals can be made in minutes and is infinitely expandable – our favourite is from an American recipe which found its way into Molly's mother's notebook via a great aunt who was sent to America at the turn of the century on an extended visit to remove her from the attentions of an unwelcome suitor.

 # Corn Fritters

Preparation time: 5 minutes
Cooking time: 8 minutes

This recipe can be extended by using a large tin of corn, adding a little more flour or a drop more milk if the mixture seems too stiff. It always turns out fine.

Imperial (Metric)

3 tablespoons flour
1 egg
½ pint (275 ml) milk
small tin corn kernels
pinch salt
3 tablespoons grated cheese

American

3 tablespoons flour
1 egg
1⅓ cups milk
small tin corn kernels
pinch salt
3 tablespoons grated cheese

Mix all ingredients together and drop heaped spoonsful into frying pan greased with a little oil. Flatten each fritter with spatula and cook for three or four minutes each side until golden brown. Serve with tomato sauce. If you make more than you can use, the fritters freeze well, packed six at a time to a plastic bag.

Variations
1. Add a slice of diced corn beef instead of corn.
2. Replace corn by 1 large grated potato and 1 small grated onion.

The smallest size tins of salmon or tuna are invaluable store cupboard items for quick tasty meals for one or two. Try this quick fish crumble.

 # Salmon or Tuna Crumble

Preparation time: 10 minutes
Cooking time: 15 minutes

Imperial (Metric)

1 small tin salmon or tuna
1 small packet crisps
a few mushrooms
½ pint (275 ml) white sauce
3 oz (75 g) plain flour
2 oz (50 g) margarine
salt and pepper

American

1 small tin salmon or tuna
1 small packet potato chips
a few mushrooms
1⅓ cups white sauce
¾ cup all purpose flour
¼ cup margarine
salt and pepper

Flake the fish and put in an ovenproof dish. Sauté the mushrooms and put on top of the fish. Make the white sauce and pour over fish. Make crumble topping by rubbing margarine into flour then adding crushed crisps. Sprinkle over dish and add seasoning to taste. Bake in oven at 350°F/180°C/Gas Mark 4 for 15 minutes. If you are very hungry serve with triangles of toast.

This savoury dish for two also takes about 15 minutes.

 # Salmon Savoury

Preparation time: 5 minutes
Cooking time: 10 minutes

Imperial (Metric)

1 small can red salmon
4 hardboiled eggs
2 oz (50 g) grated cheese
2 tablespoons milk
1 egg, beaten

American

1 small can red salmon
4 hardboiled eggs
½ cup grated cheese
2 tablespoons milk
1 egg, beaten

Peel hardboiled eggs and cut in half lengthwise. Mash up the yolks with the salmon and fill the egg whites with the mixture. Place in a buttered ovenproof dish. Mix cheese, milk and beaten egg and pour over top. Heat through in oven to brown top.

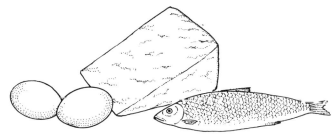

Egg and Tomato Scramble

Preparation time: 5 minutes
Cooking time: 10 minutes

This recipe is useful during the late summer tomato season and makes a very good sandwich filling as well as a hot savoury.

Imperial (Metric)
½ lb (225 g) tomatoes
4 eggs
1 oz (25 g) butter
salt and pepper
hot buttered toast

American
½ lb tomatoes
4 eggs
2 level tablespoons butter
salt and pepper
hot buttered toast

Scald and peel the tomatoes, slice them and cook gently for five minutes in the butter. Add seasoning and stir in the beaten eggs. Stir constantly over a very low heat. When the scramble is set, pile onto hot buttered toast and serve immediately.

So far the fast food we've been talking about is the sort that's useful when you come in hungry or are in hurry to catch a TV show, which when you are cooking in retirement is about as close to a genuine emergency as you want to get. It's also the sort of fast food which comes in handy if you are feeling a bit tired or under the weather and want something tasty but don't feel like spending a lot of time in the kitchen.

As a retired person you should not have any need for fast food to meet the 'unexpected guests' emergency but since this sort of fast food saved our marriage on more than one occasion, it may be as well to have a few recipes on hand, just in case.

The fact is that when I was a full-time reporter I was frequently late for meals and food was rarely made ready for the table until Molly heard my car coming up the hill. However, there were also times when I would cheerfully invite people for a meal, sometimes — but not always — phoning on my way home to let Molly know there would be guests for dinner in about half an hour.

This is not entertaining within the meaning of the act; this is a genuine emergency and here are some of the things Molly made which enabled her to play the gracious hostess and wait until the guests had gone before letting me know what she thought of me.

Pancakes

Molly can whip up a batch of pancakes by the time I have handed everyone a drink. This basic recipe makes 10 or 12 but double up the ingredients if your unexpected guests are starving.

 # Pancake Batter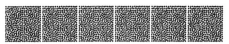

Preparation time: 10 minutes
Cooking time: 15 minutes per batch

Imperial (Metric)	American
4 oz (110g) plain flour	*1 cup all purpose flour*
1 egg	*1 egg*
½ pint (275 ml) milk	*1⅓ cups milk*
white vegetable fat for frying	*white vegetable fat for frying*

1. Stir egg and half the milk into flour and beat well until it forms a smooth batter. Leave for five minutes then beat in the rest of the milk and pour the batter into a large jug. This is much the easiest and least messy way of making pancakes.
2. Melt a little of the vegetable fat in a small frying pan and swirl it around to grease the pan. Heat until smoking then quickly pour a little batter into the middle of the pan. Tip it to spread the batter all over to make a thin pancake. Turn heat down and flip pancake over to cook the other side. Stack the pancakes in an ovenproof dish in the bottom of a low heat oven or between plates over a pan of simmering water, while you cook the rest.

Fillings
1. Spinach and cheese — Drain small can of chopped spinach, heat over low light and place a spoonful in the centre of each pancake. Add a tablespoon of grated cheese, black pepper and a sprinkling of nutmeg. Fold over pancake. Place all filled pancakes in a large ovenproof dish, sprinkle a little grated cheese over the top and brown for a minute until melted. Serve immediately.
2. Shrimp and mushroom — Drain can of shrimps and tip into small pan with contents of small tin of creamed mushrooms. Heat gently, test for seasoning. Fill and roll pancakes and serve immediately with lemon wedges.
3. Serve as a dessert after a filling soup and French bread. Either fill with jam or sprinkle with sugar and lemon juice.

 # Fondue

Preparation time: 15 minutes
Cooking time: 20 minutes

The classic fondue is made with Swiss Gruyère or Emmental but, in an emergency, Cheshire or Lancashire will melt to a reasonable consistency.

Imperial (Metric)	American
1 clove garlic	*1 clove garlic*
½ pint (275 ml) white wine or cider	*1⅓ cups white wine or cider*
1½ lb (700 g) grated cheese	*6 cups grated cheese*
2 heaped teaspoons cornflour	*2 heaped teaspoons cornstarch*
pepper and nutmeg	*pepper and nutmeg*
small glass of kirsch if available	*small glass kirsch if available*
cubes of fresh white unsliced bread	*cubes of fresh white unsliced bread*

1. If you have a fondue pan rub around the inside with the garlic then warm the wine in the pan over a low heat. Use a strong saucepan otherwise and take extra care in stirring so that the fondue doesn't stick.

2. Gradually add the cheese, stirring all the time, then when the fondue starts to bubble up add the cornflour (cornstarch) blended with either the Kirsch or a little milk. Season to taste and bring to boil again.

Hand round a basket of bread cubes and a fork for each guest. Everyone dips in a piece of bread on the end of a fork. It's as well to hand out small plates so that drips of cheese don't spatter clothes and carpets but otherwise it's a help yourself meal.

Fritters are another emergency standby — you'll find several recipes in other chapters and you'll also find that a large Spanish omelette is easily made and very filling for up to eight people.

 # Spanish Omelette

The ingredients will vary slightly according to what you have in the cupboard but you will need onions, eggs, tomatoes or ketchup (catsup) and either boiled or canned potatoes.

In a large frying pan heat a little cooking oil and lightly sauté a finely chopped onion, then add sliced cooked potatoes — small canned ones are fine — and a couple of mushrooms if you have them. Beat up at least three eggs, two teaspoons of cornflour (cornstarch) and two tablespoons of milk. Pour over the vegetables. Allow to cook for five minutes, lifting the sides of the omelette occasionally.

When the bottom is set, spread ketchup or mashed canned tomatoes over the top, sprinkle on a little grated cheese and place under grill (broiler) until top is set and golden brown. Serve immediately, cut in wedges.

With a little thought you'll be able to work out a list of emergency recipes but don't get too good at it or you may find people dropping in uninvited at meal times rather more often than you'd like!

7

Spoiling Yourself

Once word gets around that you have taken up cooking as a retirement activity you will probably have no shortage of visitors; but there will be times, however, when your partner — if you have one — is away, or when all your friends decide to go on holiday the same week.

Unfortunately, if you are anything like me, the sigh of relief you heave at having no one to please but yourself will sooner or later turn into a moan of self pity when you realise that there is no one else to appreciate your efforts — and from there it is only a step to the thought that it is hardly worth bothering.

This is the time when the rhythms of the basic routines you have established will remind you to eat and the thought that you can eat exactly the sort of food you want will help you to eat regularly. This doesn't mean that when you are on your own you have to cook monster breakfasts, immense lunches and gigantic teas and dinners — although there is nothing to stop you from doing so if you want to, apart from your own common sense.

I find that one cooked meal and a couple of snacks are about all I want to prepare when Molly is away. Mind you, as Molly doesn't care to eat meat — although she cooks it for others — I usually seize the opportunity to cook myself an occasional mixed grill for breakfast or even an Aussie steak with an egg on top and a helping of hash browns. Other days I make do with a boiled egg or maybe just cereal with toast and marmalade for breakfast, then a salad or soup or bread and cheese for lunch and treat myself by cooking a meat meal of some sort for my solitary dinner. I also find, as I have a rather sweeter tooth than Molly, that when she is away I tend to raid the freezer for things like sorbets, fruit desserts and special ice creams.

Of course a great deal depends on whether you are by yourself for just a few days, as is usually the case with me, or alone for the foreseeable future; but there is one guiding principle which applies in all cases and that is that where possible you should eat at least one decent sit-down meal every day — at mid-day or in the evening — together with a couple of snacks.

The sort of stretched meals we talked about in Chapter 3 will help — warming up a dish and perhaps adding a couple of new ingredients need only take minutes and a spoonful of cream or sherry in soups, sauces or desserts adds a special touch. Make full use, too, of the meals you have frozen on the eat-half-freeze-half principle or the meals for one such as Auntie Nell's meat pies.

Prepare really tasty snacks that you can look forward to and remember that a glass of wine or a bottle of beer with your meal isn't going to turn you into an alcoholic and could cheer you up if you are feeling low.

Approach any cooking in the spirit of adventure. I find myself doing more experimenting when Molly is away than when we are cooking together, partly because I can draw a discreet veil over any culinary disasters and partly because I tend to be more heavy handed with things like butter and cream than she does.

If our experience is anything to go by there is a temptation for people on their own — especially men— to 'pig it', as they say in Lancashire, by not setting the table properly, forgetting about napkins, using one knife for the whole meal and so on. Although I arrange my snacks on a tray, when I don't eat them in the kitchen, for my main meal of the day I set the table almost as meticulously as I would for a dinner party. I find that doing this, and using decent china instead of kitchen plates and mugs, enables me to appreciate my food even more when I'm alone and I wish I'd realised this when I was a student and sometimes ate things straight from the pan if there was no one there to see me.

Ringing the changes on snacks, experiments, frozen home cooked food and

freshly cooked meals, combined if possible with the occasional meal out, will keep alive your interest in food, especially if everything you eat is as mouthwatering as it should be.

This is the time to treat yourself — perhaps to a dish of strawberries and cream or a ripe pear poached in a tablespoon of red wine, or a pork chop cooked in cider with a sliced apple. Make a note of everything that is a great success so that you can try it out later with a friend or partner.

Even if you have a freezer full of neatly labelled main meals, you could splash out a little on starters or light meals.

Soups and Starters

Why not treat yourself to an avocado which will make two light lunches or first courses. Squeeze lemon juice over the second half and cover with cling film before putting in the refrigerator.

(Facing) **Sweets and Toffees:** Centre: Coconut Ice. Clockwise: Bonfire Treacle Toffee, Brandy Truffles — four variations, Grandma's Chocolate Tablet, Nut and Cherry Bars, Barcelona Toffee, Peppermint Creams

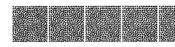 # Avocado Mousse

Preparation time: 10 minutes
No cooking

Imperial (Metric)

½ ripe avocado
1 tablespoon lemon juice
½ teaspoon Worcestershire Sauce
black pepper
1 finely chopped spring onion

American

½ ripe avocado
1 tablespoon lemon juice
½ teaspoon Worcestershire Sauce
black pepper
1 finely chopped scallion

Mash up flesh of avocado and all other ingredients. Pile back in half shell and serve with toast.

 # Avocado Salad

Cut the flesh of the other half into chunks and marinate in 1 tablespoon French dressing together with 6 thin slices of mushroom and a teaspoon of chopped chives. Pile back into half shell and decorate with a few tinned prawns if liked.

You could use the rest of the prawns to make a seafood omelette, or you could serve the prawns in sauce on toast.

The following cheese dish was a favourite of Molly's mother who often made it for herself and also found it was a much appreciated first course when she had guests.

 # Cheese Timbale (for one)

Preparation time: 10 minutes
Cooking time: 20 minutes

Imperial (Metric)

2 eggs, separated
¼ pint (150 ml) milk
1 oz (25 g) grated cheese
2 heaped tablespoons breadcrumbs
salt and pepper

American

2 eggs, separated
just over ½ cup milk
¼ cup grated cheese
2 heaped tablespoons breadcrumbs
salt and pepper

(Facing) **Biscuits:** Back: Cherry Biscuits. Clockwise: Shortbread, Chocolate Sponge Fingers, Almond Biscuits, Crunch Biscuits, Nut Biscuits, Custard Creams, Ginger Biscuits, Raisin Biscuits

1. Beat egg yolks, add milk, breadcrumbs, seasoning and cheese.
2. Beat egg whites until stiff and fold into mixture.
3. Turn into greased ovenproof dish and set in a shallow dish of hot water. Bake on the middle shelf at 375°F/190°C/Gas Mark 5 for about 20 minutes until firm. Serve at once.

 # Seafood Omelette

Preparation time: 15 minutes
Cooking time: 10 minutes

Omelette (for one)

Imperial (Metric)

2 eggs
1 tablespoon water
¾ oz (15 g) butter

American

2 eggs
1 tablespoon water
1½ level tablespoons butter

Seafood Filling

a few cooked shelled prawns
1 tablespoon chopped parsley
slice of lemon
a little parsley or onion sauce

a few cooked shelled prawns
1 tablespoon chopped parsley
slice of lemon
a little parsley or onion sauce

If you don't feel like preparing sauce just for one person this is the time to use half or even a quarter of packet sauce. The most reliable are parsley or onion. Make up according to instructions – you simply add milk – and add a little fresh chopped parsley or chives if possible.

1. Use a 6 inch (15.5 cm) pan. Break the eggs into a basin and whip lightly with a fork, then add the water and stir.
2. Heat the omelette pan over a medium flame, then drop in the knob of butter, turn up the heat and swirl the fat around to coat the pan completely. Pour in the eggs and tilt the pan to spread them, lifting the sides of the omelette regularly to allow the uncooked part to run underneath.
3. In a small pan heat your sauce and add the cooked prawns. When the omelette is set but still soft, tip the filling on top and fold the omelette over. Serve immediately.

 # Chestnut Winter Soup

Preparation time: 20 minutes
Cooking time: 50 minutes

This is an excellent winter soup when you have plenty of sprouts in the garden and chestnuts are in the shops. Freeze any surplus or refrigerate until next day.

Imperial (Metric)

½ lb (225 g) sprouts
1 small onion
1 tablespoon cooking oil
1 pint (570 ml) vegetable stock
6 oz (175 g) cooked fresh chestnuts
salt and pepper
2 tablespoons cream (optional)

American

½ lb sprouts
1 small onion
1 tablespoon cooking oil
2½ cups vegetable stock
1½ cups cooked fresh chestnuts
salt and pepper
2 tablespoons cream (optional)

1. Chop and fry the onion in the oil for five minutes. Bring stock, sprouts and chestnuts to boil and add onion. Season and simmer for 40 minutes.
2. Blend until smooth — about 30 seconds — then reheat. Serve with a swirl of cream and hot brown rolls.

Main Courses

 # Tuna Fish Bake

Preparation time: 10 minutes
Cooking time: 45 minutes

This makes a good lunch for one or can be doubled up for a starter to a larger meal for two or more.

Imperial (Metric)

1 small can tuna
1 small can condensed mushroom soup
cup breadcrumbs
1 oz (25 g) butter

American

1 small can tuna
1 small can condensed mushroom soup
cup breadcrumbs
2 level tablespoons butter

1. Butter an ovenproof dish and line with a sprinkling of breadcrumbs. Mix shredded tuna with mushroom soup and spread in dish. Put rest of breadcrumbs on top and dot with butter. Bake at 375°F/190°C/Gas Mark 5 for 45 minutes.
2. To serve with it you could thinly slice a large tomato, sprinkle with basil or mint and a teaspoon of butter and place in bottom of oven to cook at same time.

You could also bake an apple at the same time for a splendid feast. Don't forget to cut through the skin round the middle so that it won't burst and, just before serving, add a teaspoon of sherry to the brown sugar juice in the centre of the apple.

Plaice with Orange

Preparation time: 10 minutes
Cooking time: 25 minutes

This is a very fresh tasting dish and a change from the inevitable fried plaice.

Imperial (Metric)

2 small fillets of plaice
1 small orange
1 teaspoon butter
1 medium potato
salt and black pepper

American

2 small fillets of plaice
1 small orange
1 teaspoon butter
1 medium potato
salt and black pepper

1. Skin fillets, sprinkle with salt and pepper, squeeze over ½ orange. Roll up fillets and put in small ovenproof dish. Dot with butter and cover with juice from other half of orange. Cover with foil and cook at 375°F/190°C/Gas Mark 5 for 25 minutes.
2. At same time cook peeled and thinly sliced potato in top of oven on a shallow dish. Dot with butter and cook until browned.

Stuffed Eggs

Preparation time: 10 minutes
Cooking time: 7 to 10 minutes depending on egg size

This is a useful lunch or supper dish which you can adjust according to how hungry you are. Usually two eggs per person is quite enough.

Imperial (Metric)

2 hardboiled eggs
1 tablespoon plain yoghurt
½ teaspoon dry mustard
½ teaspoon Worcestershire Sauce
salt and black pepper

American

2 hardboiled eggs
1 tablespoon plain yoghurt
½ teaspoon dry mustard
½ teaspoon Worcestershire Sauce
salt and black pepper

Shell eggs and slice in half lengthwise. Carefully remove yolks and put in small basin with all other ingredients. Mash and beat until you have a smooth creamy paste. Adjust seasoning and pile into egg whites. Serve on crisp lettuce leaves. A tablespoon of cream can be added if a softer filling is required.

A tasty recipe for sausage and beans was given to us by an elderly friend who says it's always been known in his family as

 # Bachelor Bake

Preparation time: 10 minutes
Cooking time: 40 minutes

Imperial (Metric)	American
2 sausages	2 sausages
2 medium potatoes	2 medium potatoes
small can baked beans	small can baked beans
small onion	small onion
beef stock cube	beef stock cube
salt and pepper	salt and pepper

1. Grill sausages, boil potatoes and quartered onion together.
2. Slice cooked sausages and put in buttered ovenproof dish. Add beans and stock cube dissolved in a tablespoon of boiling water. Mash potatoes and onion, season with salt and pepper and spread over beans.
3. Make line on the top with a fork and bake at 425°F/220°C/Gas Mark 7 for 20 minutes until brown on top.

The same friend, Michael, produced the following two family recipes which are for just one person but can be extended when necessary.

 # Bacon and Sausage Roll

Preparation time: 5 minutes
Cooking time: 12 minutes

Imperial (Metric)	American
1 large slice of white bread	1 large slice of white bread
1 pork sausage	1 pork sausage
1 rasher bacon	1 rasher bacon
1 teaspoon butter or margarine	1 teaspoon butter or margarine

1. Grill sausage and bacon for 2 minutes. Roll bread with a heavy rolling pin until it is soft. Spread with butter or margarine.
2. Place bacon and sausage on bread and roll up. Bake on foil plate for 10 minutes at 375°F/190°C/Gas Mark 5.

Pork with Orange

Preparation time: 5 minutes, plus 3 hours marinating
Cooking time: 20 minutes

Imperial (Metric)

1 pork chop or small pork steak
1 small sweet orange

American

1 pork chop or small pork steak
1 small sweet orange

1. Squeeze juice from orange, pour over chop or steak and leave to marinate in refrigerator, for at least three hours. Turn the meat over once or twice to make sure that the juice penetrates.
2. Place on foil to catch juices while you grill (broil) the meat on both sides until browned and tender.
3. Serve with the juices. This goes well with mashed potatoes.

Croque Monsieur

Preparation time: 5 minutes
Cooking time: 6 minutes

This is also one of Michael's favourites — and one of mine.

Imperial (Metric)

2 slices white bread
2 oz (50 g) cheese in 2 slices
1 slice cooked ham
cooking oil

American

2 slices white bread
2 thin slices hard cheese
1 slice cooked ham
cooking oil

1. Make a sandwich with ham in the middle of cheese slices placed between bread. Fry in hot oil in shallow pan for three minutes each side until golden brown.
2. Eat immediately.

Salads

Don't think in terms of a limp lettuce leaf and a slice of boiled beetroot when you are planning a salad lunch. Lettuce straight from the garden is delicious, of course, but when you are on your own it's a good time to try out bean or rice salads and experiment with different dressings. Any that you particularly enjoy can be added to your collection of recipes and produced as something a little different for your partner or friends.

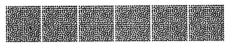 # Rainbow Beans

Preparation time: 15 minutes

Cooking time: nil with tinned beans; 10 minutes if using fresh green beans

This recipe was given to us by a Mexican friend. It is incredibly simple but looks very attractive with the different coloured beans arranged on a white dish. If you are using dried beans you will need to soak them overnight and then boil or pressure cook them next day; but for your first experiment try small tins of the beans.

Imperial (Metric)

small can white butter beans
small can red kidney beans
small can French beans or ½ lb
(225 g) fresh
French dressing with garlic
(see page 55)
tablespoon chopped chives
small lemon

American

small can white butter beans
small can red kidney beans
small can French beans or ½ lb fresh
French dressing with garlic
(see page 55)
tablespoon chopped chives
small lemon

Drain all beans, cook fresh French beans until *al dente* then drain. Arrange beans in rows or swirls, one colour at a time on a white dish. Pour over French dressing with garlic, sprinkle with chopped chives and place lemon wedges around dish.

This salad is excellent on its own but is the perfect accompaniment to a slice of ham or salami. If covered it will keep well for a couple of days in the refrigerator.

 # Apple and Avocado Salad

Preparation time: 20 minutes

Cooking time: nil

Imperial (Metric)

2 red apples
1 ripe avocado
2 oz (50 g) mushrooms
1 spring onion
lemon juice
4 oz (110 g) cooked new peas
mint dressing
lettuce leaves

American

2 red apples
1 ripe avocado
2 oz mushrooms
1 scallion
lemon juice
4 oz cooked new peas
mint dressing
lettuce leaves

1. Slice apples — with peel — and cover with a little lemon juice. Chop flesh of avocado into small chunks and mix with apple. Add thinly sliced mushrooms, chopped spring onion (scallion) and peas.
2. Add a little mint dressing, mix thoroughly and pile into dish lined with lettuce leaves or any available green salad.

Chicken Rice Salad

Preparation time: 20 minutes
Cooking time: 25 minutes if using white rice, 45 if using brown

This was a favourite with Molly's mother — it's light and tasty and just right for a summer meal when you want something between a snack and a substantial dinner.

Imperial (Metric)	American
(for one)	*(for one)*
2 oz (50 ml) uncooked rice	*¼ cup uncooked rice*
5 fluid oz (150 ml) chicken stock or cube and water	*just over ½ cup chicken stock or cube and water*
1 small breast chicken	*1 small breast chicken*
teaspoon turmeric	*teaspoon turmeric*
1 oz (25 g) raisins	*2 tablespoons raisins*
grated rind and juice of 1 lemon	*grated rind and juice of 1 lemon*
2 teaspoons flaked almonds	*2 teaspoons flaked almonds*
3 teaspoons butter	*3 teaspoons butter*

1. Melt 1 teaspoon butter in a heavy-bottomed saucepan. Add rice and stir for a minute then add chicken stock and bring to boil. Put lid on and turn down to simmer. Leave for 20 minutes (40 if you are using brown rice).

Meanwhile cut the chicken into small dice and fry quickly in a little butter. Uncover rice which should have absorbed all the stock. Stir in chicken and turmeric.

2. Tip into serving bowl, add raisins and juice and rind of 1 lemon. Leave to cool. Scatter flaked almonds on top before serving.

You can easily adjust the quantities if you want to offer this to more people and it is a useful item for picnics and buffet suppers.

Variation
Add thin slices of red and green peppers or thinly sliced raw mushrooms marinated in French dressing.

I love to experiment with desserts when Molly is out or away and many of my efforts have now found their way into our regular menus. One of the easiest has a beautifully refreshing taste.

Orange and Lemon (for one person)

Preparation time: 5 minutes plus cooling time
Cooking time: 10 minutes

Imperial (Metric)	American
1 large sweet orange	*1 large sweet orange*
2 teaspoons caster sugar	*2 teaspoons caster sugar*

2 tablespoons lemon juice
1 tablespoon water
1 tablespoon caster sugar
1 teaspoon orange liqueur or sherry

2 tablespoons lemon juice
1 tablespoon water
1 tablespoon caster sugar
1 teaspoon orange liqueur or sherry

1. Peel and thinly slice orange. Arrange in a dish and sprinkle with 2 teaspoons caster sugar.
2. Boil lemon juice, water and tablespoon caster sugar until syrupy (about 10 minutes). Pour over orange slices and leave to cool.
3. Just before serving add a teaspoon of sherry or orange liqueur.

This is just a treat for yourself but you can easily extend the recipe and the same applies to the following luxury pudding.

Ginger Cream Log (for one person)

Preparation time: 15 minutes plus refrigerator time
No cooking

Imperial (Metric)

6 ginger biscuits (see p. 140)
1 tablespoon strawberry jam
1 tablespoon sherry
small carton whipping cream

American

6 ginger biscuits (see p. 140)
1 tablespoon strawberry jam
1 tablespoon sherry
1/2 cup heavy cream

1. Pour sherry into small dish and dip each biscuit briefly in sherry on both sides. Smear with jam and press biscuits together in turn in a log shape. Place on a plate.
2. Whip cream until thick then cover the log and refrigerate for at least half an hour.

This is so good you'll wonder why you ever wanted to try anything else.

Variations

Lemon curd or raspberry jam are equally good.

Packet jellies (jello) are particularly useful if you regard them as ingredients in a recipe and get away from the nursery jelly and custard image. We like to make up a pint of, say, raspberry or lime, allow it to cool, then fill four small yoghurt or cream containers and add a different fresh fruit to each. Grated apple, raspberries of course, sections of orange, a chopped plum — cover the tops, keep them in the refrigerator and you have a pudding ready at any time. If you like to take the trouble to set a small piece of sponge cake in the bottom and add a little cream to the top of the container just before serving you have a ready-made trifle.

Jenny, one of our friends who is herself retired, gave us this recipe for a more sophisticated jelly.

 # Orange Coffee Jelly

Preparation time: 10 minutes
Cooking time: nil

Imperial (Metric)

1 packet orange jelly
1 pint (570 ml) strong black coffee
1 small sweet orange

American

1 packet orange jello or crystals
2½ cups strong black coffee
1 small sweet orange

Make coffee (instant is fine) and pour over separated jelly (jello) segments or crystals. Stir until dissolved. Pour into small moulds and when almost set firm arrange segments of fresh orange on top.

Variation

Finely grated orange peel and a teaspoon of finely grated dark chocolate is a pleasant alternative.

Ice Cream

We always like to keep a container of vanilla ice cream in the freezer to go with soft fruit or to make up a variety of desserts. You probably already have a good recipe but here are two of our standbys.

 # Basic Vanilla Ice Cream

Total preparation time: 40 minutes
Cooking time: 20 minutes

Imperial (Metric)

1 pint (570 ml) fresh milk
2 eggs, separated
8 oz (225 g) caster sugar
1 teaspoon vanilla essence
½ pint (275 ml) whipping cream

American

2½ cups fresh milk
2 eggs, separated
1 cup caster sugar
1 teaspoon vanilla essence
1⅓ cups heavy cream

1. Heat milk to boiling point. Put sugar and egg yolks in a bowl and beat until smooth, then add 3 tablespoons of hot milk. Beat in the rest of the milk then pour into a double saucepan – with boiling water in the base pan – and reheat, stirring all the time until the cream is thick enough to coat the spoon.
2. Leave to cool then add the vanilla essence. Beat egg whites stiffly and fold into the mixture. Whip cream and stir in.
3. Pour into freezer containers, cover and freeze until mushy. Remove and stir well twice before leaving to freeze completely.

Custard Ice Cream

Preparation time: 15 minutes
Cooking time: 20 minutes

Imperial (Metric)	American
1½ pints (850 ml) fresh milk	3¾ cups fresh milk
1 oz (25 g) custard powder	1 heaped tablespoon custard powder
4 oz (110 g) caster sugar	4 level tablespoons caster sugar
2 eggs, separated	2 eggs, separated
1 teaspoon vanilla essence	1 teaspoon vanilla essence
¼ pint (150 ml) whipping cream	just over ½ cup heavy cream

1. Mix egg yolks, sugar and custard powder with a little of the cold milk until smooth. Heat the rest of the milk to below boiling and stir it into the mixture. Return all the custard to the pan (a double boiler is best but otherwise stir carefully) and bring very gradually to the boil, stirring all the time until it thickens. Stir in the vanilla essence and leave in the pan to cool. Press a piece of greaseproof paper down onto the surface of the custard to stop a skin forming.
2. When the custard is quite cold, fold in whisked egg whites and cream. Put into a large freezer container or half a dozen small ones — we find the latter more convenient. Cover containers. You don't need to stir this ice cream half way through. It keeps well for up to three months.

One of our favourite recipes using vanilla ice cream is to mix a few spoonfuls with the juice of half an orange and decorate the top with grated rind. Simple, but delicious.

In the soft fruit season we fill the freezer with an assortment of home-made fruit ices, sorbets and purées until we wonder how we'll ever get through them, but it is amazing how many people seem to sense that we've just made their special favourite. All the small cartons that have taken up so much space in the kitchen cupboards for months are suddenly useful items in great demand because, although we fill large plastic containers to use when family and friends come to meals, we find the one, two or four portion size tubs invaluable. The labelling and filling takes a bit longer but the ices are ready for the table much quicker and if you've ever tried to hack off pieces of strawberry ice from a 5lb container you'll know exactly what I mean.

Follow the directions for Strawberry Sorbet (see page 27) to make Raspberry, Loganberry or Blackberry Sorbet but pass the fruit purée through a sieve after blending so that you can get rid of the seeds.

Raspberry Ice Cream

Preparation time: 20 minutes
Cooking time: nil

This is one of our summer favourites.

Imperial (Metric)
1 lb (450 g) fresh raspberries
8 oz (225 g) caster sugar
1 pint (570 ml) double cream
juice of 1 orange

American
1 lb fresh raspberries
1 cup caster sugar
2½ cups heavy cream
juice of 1 orange

1. Blend raspberries and then pass through a sieve to remove seeds.
2. Mix the purée with the sugar and orange juice and chill for an hour. (You can freeze purée at this stage in small containers to use with yoghurt or plain ice cream — we usually do this with a batch of raspberries and strawberries.)
3. Whip the cream, fold into the purée and freeze. Remove after a couple of hours and stir the frozen bits from the sides. Put into different size containers, cover and freeze.

Blackcurrant Ice Cream

Preparation time: 20 minutes
Cooking time: 10 minutes

This a different type of recipe, using eggs.

Imperial (Metric)
1 lb (450 g) blackcurrants
8 oz (225 g) caster sugar
1 pint (570 ml) double cream
4 eggs, separated

American
1 lb blackcurrants
1 cup caster sugar
2½ cups heavy cream
4 eggs, separated

1. Slowly cook the blackcurrants in a tablespoon of water then sieve and allow to cool.
2. Beat the cream until it stands up in peaks, whisk egg yolks and combine with cream. Stir into purée.
3. Whip egg whites with sugar and fold into purée. Put into large plastic container, cover and put in deep freeze for two or three hours. Take out to stir and then pot in a variety of containers.

Initially some of these ice creams might seem expensive because of the price of cream, but the recipes make quite a large quantity and the flavour is really exceptional.

Experiment with different fruits, using some of these recipes as your basis.

When it comes to sorbets the possibilities are endless. We used to make fruit ones years ago when we lived at the farm but the leaf sorbets were something we came across only a few years ago when Molly's mother found a recipe for Poor Parson's Water Ice. We thought it was unique but since then we have come across many variations, all with an ecclesiastical flavour — Rectory Water Ice, Church Sorbet and so on.

 ## Poor Parson's Water Ice

Preparation time: 20 minutes plus overnight infusion
Cooking time: 5 minutes

Imperial (Metric)

1 pint (570 ml) water
8 oz (225 g) caster sugar
1 egg white
a large handful of young blackcurrant
* leaves*

American

2½ cups water
1 cup caster sugar
1 egg white
a large handful of young blackcurrant
* leaves*

Put sugar and water in a pan and heat until sugar dissolves. Wash blackcurrant leaves quickly under cold water to remove any dust then put in a large crock or bowl. Pour sugar water over them, cover with a clean cloth and leave overnight to infuse. Strain off next day, put in a large container and freeze. After a couple of hours stir the water ice and fold in the stiffly whipped egg white. Spoon into small containers and freeze. Serve in glass coupes with a few mint leaves or a couple of blackcurrants cooked in sugar syrup.

There are many variations on leaf sorbets — we have tried lemon balm and peppermint with equal success. They are wonderfully refreshing and the sort of thing that you cannot buy.

 ## Brown Bread Ice Cream

Preparation time: 20 minutes
Cooking time: 10 minutes

This has been a favourite since Victorian times but most people seem surprised when they discover what it's made of. This version doesn't need stirring part way through freezing so you can put it straight into small containers.

Imperial (Metric)

8 oz (225 g) fresh wholemeal
* breadcrumbs*

American

2 cups fresh wholemeal breadcrumbs
1½ cups soft brown sugar

4 oz (110 g) soft brown sugar	1⅓ cups light cream
½ pint single cream	2 eggs, separated
2 eggs, separated	1 tablespoon brandy
1 tablespoon brandy	1⅓ cups heavy cream
½ pint (275 ml) double cream	

1. Crisp the breadcrumbs in the top of a moderate oven until they are slightly brown.
2. Whip double cream then add to single cream, egg yolks and sugar. Whisk together thoroughly then stir in brandy and breadcrumbs.
3. Whisk egg whites until stiff and fold into mixture. Freeze until required.

Variations
A few ground walnuts added at the same time as the breadcrumbs increases the nutty flavour and we have found that rum, instead of brandy, plus a tablespoon of grated orange rind, is another delicious alternative.

 Cassata

Preparation time: 45 minutes

Cooking time: nil

Every Italian restaurant has its own version of cassata but our own recipe always finds favour with guests. We use a square container of home-made vanilla ice cream, but it's good with any block of plain ice cream. Make sure to assemble your other ingredients before taking the ice cream out of the freezer because it has to be hard enough to slice.

Imperial (Metric)	**American**
large block of vanilla ice cream	large block of vanilla ice cream
4 oz (110 g) chopped walnuts	1 cup chopped walnuts
2 oz (50 g) chopped seedless raisins	½ cup chopped seedless raisins
2 oz (50 g) dark chocolate, grated	¼ cup grated dark chocolate
1 oz (25 g) chopped glacé cherries	2 tablespoons chopped glacé cherries
2 tablespoons brandy or sherry	2 tablespoons brandy or sherry

1. Assemble ingredients in small bowls. Pour brandy or sherry over raisins and walnuts and leave to marinate for half an hour.
2. Place ice cream block on a cold slab and slice through into six or eight sections. Spoon fruits, nuts and chocolate between each slice, press together and slide back into container before the ice cream has a chance to melt. Put back in freezer until required.

This is very rich and you will only be able to eat a small amount, but it is a very attractive finish to a dinner party, especially if you grate more chocolate over the top before serving. I always put some in a small pot to cheer up a meal on my own.

Less rich but equally attractive are the summer fruit mousses which can be made from any fruit purée and curd cheese. We make these regularly during the year with fresh fruit or with frozen fruit purée. You simply use curd cheese and half the quantity of fruit purée, mash together until smooth, then put in a dish and chill. If you have a little of the fresh fruit you can decorate the top. This won't freeze but it keeps for a couple of days in the refrigerator.

My special chocolate mousse is so rich that I make it only on very special occasions and serve it in tiny dishes.

Special Chocolate Mousse

Preparation time: 10 minutes
Cooking time: 5 minutes

Imperial (Metric)

4 oz (110 g) plain dark chocolate
2 oz (50 g) ground almonds
4 oz (110 g) caster sugar
4 oz (110 g) butter
4 oz (110 g) ginger biscuits, finely
*   ground*
tablespoon milk
teaspoon ginger
dessertspoon rum

American

¼ lb dark chocolate
½ cup ground almonds
½ cup caster sugar
½ cup butter
¼ lb ginger biscuits, finely ground
tablespoon milk
teaspoon ginger
dessertspoon rum

Melt chocolate and butter in a bowl over pan of hot water, beat in sugar and all other ingredients until you have a smooth chocolate cream. Quickly spoon into small dishes or one large serving bowl and refrigerate until needed.

This is splendid on its own but becomes a definite party dish when served with a rum cream sauce. This is simply thick whipping cream with a spoonful of rum beaten in − 1 tablespoon to ½ pint of cream − and a little grated chocolate. When you have tasted this you will understand why it's only usually served about once a year!

Getting away from cold summer desserts, one of my favourite puddings when I'm on my own is Caramelised Bananas. They are easy and quick to make and if the bananas are very ripe you can mash them up with the sugar and they still taste marvellous.

 # Caramelised Bananas (for one)

Preparation time: 5 minutes
Cooking time: 5 minutes

Imperial (Metric)	**American**
1 banana	*1 banana*
1 oz (25 g) caster sugar	*1 level tablespoon caster sugar*
pinch ginger	*pinch ginger*

1. Mix the ginger and sugar. Peel banana and slice in two lengthways. Place on foil dish, cover with sugar and put under grill (broiler) until caramelised.

Variations
1. Serve with vanilla ice cream beaten with ginger syrup.
2. Add a spoonful of rum to sugar.
3. Substitute thin slices of apple for banana.

As well as asking friends for recipes, you could find a good source in old cookery books. Molly's mother's 1937 *Household Guide* is in constant use and we were recently lent an old book by a friend in her eighties. This contains '1000 Tested and Inexpensive Recipes' proving that all old cookery books do not start with 'Take 5 lbs sweet butter'.

 # Baked Custard

Preparation time: 5 minutes
Cooking time: 20−30 minutes

This is a perfect dish to put in the bottom of the oven when you are cooking something else. You can also use it as the filling for custard tarts in a pastry case.

Imperial (Metric)	**American**
2 eggs	*2 eggs*
1 pint (570 ml) milk	*2½ cups milk*
1 oz (25 g) caster sugar	*1 level tablespoon caster sugar*
nutmeg (optional)	*nutmeg (optional)*

Beat the eggs, add the sugar and milk and stir well. Pour into a pie dish and bake in a slow oven till set. Sprinkle the top with a little nutmeg if liked, when almost set.

(Facing) **Sweet Pastries:** Eccles Cakes, Treacle Tart, Bakewell Tart, Cheesecake

Cousin Norah's Baked Orange Custard (for one)

Preparation time: 5 minutes
Cooking time: 15−25 minutes

We found this on a browning scrap of paper in Molly's mother's notebook and have used it many times. It's one of those useful puddings to fill shelf space when you are baking or cooking a casserole. Double up the ingredients for two.

Imperial (Metric)	**American**
½ pint (275 ml) milk	*1⅓ cups milk*
teaspoon cornflour	*teaspoon cornstarch*
1 egg	*1 egg*
1 tablespoon orange marmalade	*1 tablespoon orange marmalade*
1 tablespoon caster sugar	*1 tablespoon caster sugar*

Blend cornflour to a paste with a little of the milk. Whisk together with all the other ingredients and turn into a greased pie dish. Bake in the bottom of a moderate oven until set.

The main thing when cooking for yourself is to enjoy it and to enjoy what you cook. And, of course, when something new turns out to be a great success, put the recipe in your notebook so that you can share it with your partner or friends.

(Facing) **Savoury Pies:** Steak and Kidney Pie, Nini's Fish Pie, Cheese and Onion Pie

8

Aiming for the Hundred

Let's face it, if you have made it to retirement age — even early retirement age — without too many major health disasters you must have been doing something right, or at least nothing too drastically wrong. However, now that you have the time to select and prepare your food it's a bit easier to make sure you have healthy meals than it was when you were working and had to think in terms of speed and convenience.

This doesn't mean that you have to 'go on a diet' as such but when it comes to doing your best to ensure a long and healthy life you can get more mileage out of better fuel — and, after all, we are aiming to be cooking at a hundred.

One really great thing about retirement is that eating in retirement will almost certainly be healthier than eating while at work, without your having to do a thing about it. For instance, you will probably eat fewer café, restaurant or canteen meals — all of which can be deadly in their way — and more wholesome, home-cooked dishes. At the same time, now that the pressure is off, instead of bolted breakfasts or lightning lunches there should be the sort of tranquil feeding which, especially if combined with a gentle daily stroll — for which you now also have time — is a positive aid to digestion.

You may well think that bolting down food is an easy habit to break but it's about as difficult as giving up cigarettes and can be just as beneficial. Even now, decades after I gave up working to a strict timetable, Molly has still to remind herself not to eat on the run, a habit she acquired because she was the one who prepared and served food for me when I was in a hurry, as well as eating her own meal.

Of course no one's suggesting that we should chew every mouthful thirty-two times in the way which is reputed to have made Mr Gladstone such an unpopular table companion, but you can and should take things a little slower than you did.

Another benefit of cooking in retirement is that you should need very little convenience food, much of which is less than nutritious and some of which is positively harmful. It's fair to assume that if the list of ingredients printed on the can or packet reads like a foundation course in chemistry, it could be unwise to make the food in question a regular part of your diet.

However, junk foods in small quantities won't kill you — otherwise the streets of our major towns and cities would be littered with bodies — and there is a world of difference between eating the occasional item and becoming a junk food junkie. Unless you are allergic to it, don't get too upset if something you buy contains monosodium glutamate or somebody serves you a snack which has obviously come straight from a laboratory; now that you are retired you will be eating so much good stuff most of the time that the odd item of plastic food shouldn't make any difference – except to your taste buds.

The Lees Law of Nourishment works like Gresham's Law in reverse and states categorically that 'Good food drives out bad' and the more good food you cook for yourself the less bad food you buy. This means that, provided you remember not to eat food with lots of additives on a regular basis, you can let the Law work for you and concentrate on other aspects of healthy eating.

For one thing, while many of us eat a great deal too much, others eat too little for their health and retirement does give us a chance to get things right – or at least a little better. In this respect I have to confess that, unfortunately, I fall into the first category with an appetite which, if unrestrained, would make Gargantua seem like an anorexic. I blame the long-term effects of wartime shortages which, I claim, make me guzzle to compensate, but Molly insists that it's nothing but greed. Whatever the truth of the matter I think it's one of life's major ironies that no sooner can you afford a decent meal than you find you have reached the age where you put on weight.

Not so long ago I became not merely plump but immensely fat, an eighteen stone weakling who doctors were beginning to refer to as obese. Thanks to a lifetime of Press lunches, business dinners and drinks with the lads I was, not to put too fine a point on it, a mess. And while I knew I had to do something about it I also knew there was no way I was going to live on lettuce leaves and lemon juice for the rest of my life, or spend most of my free time 'going for the burn'.

I've told the story of exactly what I did about it and how I lost 56 lbs in three months without giving up the good things of life in *The Champagne Fitness Book* (Redcliffe Press), but the basic principle will be of interest to most people cooking in retirement, especially those like me who start to look like a tyre ad. after only a few beers.

The principle is that it is much better for you to eat and drink modest amounts of high quality food and wine than it is to consume great quantities of cheap stodge and low priced drinks that pile on the weight.

By choosing to eat and drink high quality – and therefore perhaps higher priced food, your wallet, unless you are a multi-millionaire, becomes a restricting factor and you spend roughly the same amount but eat less.

On the other hand, because you have substituted the best of food and drink for the not so good, you won't feel deprived or bored, which is where most diets fall down. For instance, although 'Champagne' fitness refers as much to the pleasure of waking up in the morning feeling terrific as it does to the bubbly itself, there's no doubt that a glass of Champagne helps you to bear the absence of large quantities of beer and spirits with a certain amount of fortitude.

If you need to lose a great deal of weight you would be well advised to consult your doctor, as I did, before going on a diet or starting any more strenuous exercising than you have been used to. If, like most people, you only need to lose a few pounds, then retirement is the ideal time to do it as you are in a position to

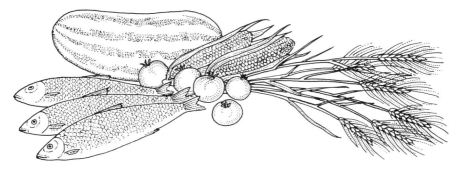

choose what you eat without the pressures or temptations most full-time workers have to contend with.

Incidentally, while I was working on *Champagne Fitness* I discovered that diet is yet another word which seems to have earned itself a bad reputation. Diet, I found, originally had nothing to do with restrictions or sacrifice but came from a Greek word meaning choice.

That being the case, should you choose to eat food which will help you to lose weight here are a few things you may care to try.

Meals to Make You Feel Champagne Fit — and How to Cook Them

These are complete menus for a day, totalling only 1,000 calories. *Starred recipes are given in detail.

Menu 1

Breakfast (200 calories)
4 oz (110 g) grilled kipper
small slice brown bread
tea or coffee with skimmed milk

Lunch (270 calories)
Stuffed tomatoes* with watercress salad* (115 calories)
Peaches in natural juice with spoonful plain yoghurt (55)
Glass red wine (100)

Dinner (500 calories)
4 oz (110 g) (¼ lb) each of grilled bacon steak, steamed sea kale or Swiss chard,
  broad beans, small new potatoes (total 270)
8 oz (225 g) ½ lb fresh raspberries (60) with 2 tablespoons single (light) cream (60)
Glass red wine (100)
Coffee with skimmed milk

 # Stuffed Tomatoes
(115 calories with watercress salad)

Preparation time: 5 minutes
Cooking time: 5 minutes

Imperial (Metric)

2 average sized tomatoes
1 oz (25 g) Cheshire cheese, grated
black pepper
fresh basil

American

2 average sized tomatoes
4 tablespoons grated cheese
black pepper
fresh basil

Cut tomatoes in half horizontally and scoop out flesh. Mix thoroughly with most of the grated cheese, plus pepper and basil. Pile back into tomato skins, scatter rest of cheese on top and grill (broil) until cheese bubbles and browns slightly. Serve with watercress salad.

Watercress Salad

Preparation time: 5 minutes
Cooking time: nil

Imperial (Metric)

1 bunch watercress
juice and grated rind of 1 lemon
black pepper
dessertspoon plain yoghurt

American

1 bunch watercress
juice and grated rind of 1 lemon
black pepper
dessertspoon plain yoghurt

1. Wash watercress carefully and discard any woody stems.
2. Squeeze lemon juice over it just before serving and serve with dish of yoghurt mixed with black pepper and lemon rind.

Menu 2

Breakfast (175 calories)
½ grapefruit
2 small slices brown bread toasted, with scraping low fat spread and teaspoon marmalade (150)
tea or coffee with skimmed milk

Lunch (365 calories)
6 oz (175 g) trout with large serving green beans and 2 grilled tomatoes (185)
5 oz (150 g) plain yoghurt with juice and grated peel of orange or lemon (80), add sweetener if required
Glass white wine (100)

Dinner (460 calories)
2 oz (50 g) (1 slice) lamb's liver, 1 rasher lean back bacon, 2 grilled tomatoes (200 calories total)
4 oz (110 g) (¼ lb) broad beans (50)
cherry curd pudding* (110)
Glass red wine (100)

Cherry Curd Pudding (110 calories)

Preparation time: 10 minutes
Cooking time: nil

Imperial (Metric)

3 oz (75 g) sweet black cherries
2 oz (50 g) curd cheese
sachet of sweetener if required

American

just under 1 cup sweet black cherries
¼ cup curd cheese
sachet or 2 teaspoons sweetener
*   if required*

1. Stone and chop cherries, reserving 3 for decoration.

2. Mash sweetener if used into cheese and beat in cherries thoroughly. Pile into small serving dish and decorate with whole cherries.

This is a particularly rich tasting, although low calorie, pudding.

Variations
Use the same quantity of other fruits such as strawberries, raspberries, blackcurrants or blackberries. They are equally delicious.

Menu 3

Breakfast (195 calories)
4 oz (110 ml) (½ cup) tomato juice (25)
breakfast pizza* (170 calories)

Lunch (346 calories)
eggs in onion sauce* (156)
½ lb (225 g) fresh strawberries with 1 tablespoon double (heavy) cream (90 calories)
glass Champagne (100)

Dinner (470 calories)
3 oz (75 g) (under ¼ lb) fillet steak grilled (broiled) with large helping spinach and
*   8 oz (225 g) (½ lb) tiny button mushrooms in red wine sauce* (total dish 260*
*   calories — mushrooms alone, 65 per serving)*
Glass red wine (100)
Lime sorbet* (110)

 Breakfast Pizza (170 calories)

Preparation time: 5 minutes
Cooking time: 5 minutes

Imperial (Metric)	**American**
1 small slice toast	*1 small slice toast*
1 tablespoon ketchup	*1 tablespoon catsup*
3 anchovies	*3 anchovies*
½ teaspoon oregano	*½ teaspoon oregano*
½ oz (10 g) grated cheese	*2 tablespoons grated cheese*

Spread toast with tomato ketchup (catsup), cut anchovies into strips and place on top. Sprinkle with oregano and cheese. Grill (broil) until cheese bubbles.

Eggs in Onion Sauce (156 calories)

Preparation time: 15 minutes
Cooking time: 30 minutes

Imperial (Metric)

1 hardboiled egg
1 large onion
2 fl oz (55 ml) milk
2 fl oz (55 ml) water
2 teaspoons cornflour
salt and pepper

American

1 hardboiled egg
1 large onion
just over 1/4 cup milk
just over 1/4 cup water
2 teaspoons cornstarch
salt and pepper

1. Shell and cut egg in half lengthwise. Place cut side down in small greased ovenproof dish. Boil and mash onion.
2. Make a sauce with milk, water and cornflour (cornstarch), add onions, season to taste and pile over egg. Heat in oven or under grill for few minutes. An additional 10 calories if you add a sprinkling of Parmesan.

Mushrooms in Red Wine Sauce (65 calories)

Preparation time: 2 minutes
Cooking time: 10 minutes

Imperial (Metric)

8 oz (225 g) tiny button mushrooms
1 tablespoon water
1 tablespoon red wine
1 teaspoon cornflour
1/2 teaspoon each low fat spread, soy sauce, Worcestershire Sauce and chopped chives
1/2 bouillon cube
pepper and salt

American

1/2 lb tiny button mushrooms
1 tablespoon water
1 tablespoon red wine
1 teaspoon cornstarch
1/2 teaspoon each low fat spread, soy sauce, Worcestershire Sauce and chopped chives
1/2 bouillon cube
pepper and salt

1. Poach mushrooms in salted water for one minute then drain.
2. Mix sauce by heating red wine, water, mix in cornflour and add all other ingredients.
3. Add mushrooms and cook gently for five minutes.

 # Lime Sorbet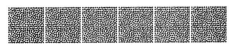

Preparation time: 10 minutes
Cooking time: 5 minutes

Recipe is for four portions. Pour into four small containers after final whisk.

Imperial (Metric)

4 limes
4 oz (110 g) granulated sugar
1 pint (570 ml) water
2 egg whites

American

4 limes
4 level tablespoons granulated sugar
2½ cups water
2 egg whites

1. Finely grate rind of limes, add to water with juice of fruit.
2. Heat to boiling point them remove from heat and stir in sugar until dissolved. Freeze until mushy in one container.
3. Turn out into bowl, whisk well and fold in beaten whites of eggs. Pour into four small containers and freeze.

Putting on Weight

Alas, the need to put on weight has never been one of my problems and though it was once one of Molly's — who was thin as a lath when we married — such is not now the case. However, I do appreciate that being too thin is as much of a problem as being too fat and while you should consult your doctor if you suffer a rapid and inexplicable weight loss, cooking in retirement should help if you merely want to add a few pounds.

With a bit of luck retirement itself will remove some of the stress factors that may have been causing sleeplessness, loss of appetite and loss of weight and this might be all you need to put you on the road to your ideal weight.

At the same time, spending an hour or so a day pottering in the kitchen garden, doing your planned shopping, going fishing or strolling around country lanes on the look out for blackberries and other free food will probably give you a better appetite than you've had for years. Add to this the fact that the meals you cook in retirement are going to be pretty mouthwatering anyway, and the chances are that you will begin to gain weight appreciably. Don't be over enthusiastic though as you don't want to get fat and doctors agree that it's fractionally better to be underweight than overweight, although a swing of a few pounds either side of your ideal weight is nothing to worry about.

If you enjoy a drink, a couple of glasses of wine or a glass of stout each day could help those who need a few more pounds. We even helped to cure a young anorexic friend of ours by giving her a glass of home-made egg-nog every time we saw her. Made with eggs, cream, sugar and cream sherry, mixed in a blender, the drink didn't seem like food to her — especially as she was young enough to consider alcohol deliciously wicked — but it was in fact stuffed with calories.

The basic rules of weight gain and weight loss are boringly simple, namely that if you eat more than you need you will put on weight and if you eat less than you need you will lose.

The trouble is that as we get older most of us need less calories than we did when we were young while our eating habits tend to remain the same. For years our desk bound, bench bound, television bound bodies are stuffed with the same amount of food and drink we consumed as hyper-active teenagers — perhaps even more, as teenagers often skip meals simply because they are enjoying themselves.

Fortunately, retirement is the easiest time to change our eating habits and changing our eating habits is a hundred times easier than going on a diet.

Let's for example, take a quick look at a few items we can cut down on or cut out while cooking in retirement and what we can hope to achieve without dieting.

We could, for instance, change from canned fruit in heavy syrup to fresh fruit or fruit canned in its own or other fruit juice without added sugar.

Molly and I discovered that we now prefer the taste of unsweetened fruit canned in its own juice to the other sort — which is a bonus — and we've also swapped from butter to a low fat spread, except when we're eating bread and butter on its own, in which case we use the unsalted kind.

Using a calorie counter, work out your current calorie intake for a week and if you are strictly honest — and overweight — this could give you a shock.

Taking It Easy

If you simply change sugar for sweetener you lose about 1,000 calories a week, just knock out one pint of beer a week and you save more than 200, and so on until you have achieved a regular saving of 1,750 calories a week which should result in a weight loss of half a pound a week — or 26 lb in a year — without your having to do much about it. Of course the loss won't be sudden and dramatic but, after all, you do have the time to take it easy and if you are in a hurry — and your doctor approves — you could always try *Champagne Fitness*.

Additives and Preservatives

While weight is an important factor in achieving and maintaining good health, especially as we get a bit older, it's far from being the whole story and, as we have seen, there are things like additives and preservatives that we have to be careful about.

In small quantities these are relatively harmless and can usually be avoided merely by reading the labels and steering away from chemicals whenever we can. Many supermarkets are actively helping you to do this now by labelling many items 'Free from Preservatives and Artificial Colourings' but in many ways there is more danger in the things we habitually consume without being really aware of them — like salt and fats.

Salts and Fats

In the case of salt, most of us get through many times more than we need and, as too much salt is harmful, it pays to take care. Fortunately, by cooking at home as opposed to buying convenience foods, it's possible to avoid a lot of the salt used for preserving cooked meats and butter or added as a taste enhancer. When cooking fresh food it is easier to control the amount of salt used and to cut it down in order to enjoy the natural taste of the food. Try not to grab the salt cellar before you reach for your fork; ten to one the food doesn't need any more salt and the gesture is merely the habit of a confirmed salt addict.

In the case of fats, it is advisable to cut down by using a spread high in polyunsaturates as they not only contain less fat but also they spread very easily so you use a lot less — especially if the butter is kept in the refrigerator and can only be put on bread in huge chunks. Keep butter for a treat — but try out the unsalted variety. If you really hate all the low fat spreads then at least keep a small quantity of your butter in a cupboard or a cool pantry so that it spreads easily and saves you both calories, fat and money.

Eat lean meat whenever possible and try to cut off most of the fat, although there is no need to get rid of it all if it's something you enjoy. Roast pork without the 'tram lines' of crisp crackling wouldn't be the same dish for me but I do restrain myself from scoffing the lot.

Moderation is hell but it's a lot better than deprivation which is why, among all the wholesome recipes in this book, you will fnd the odd piece of calorie filled wickedness.

Most of the dishes, however, make for healthy eating if only because the fresh ingredients — provided they are not cooked to death — contain all the vitamins, fibre and so on that most people are likely to need.

Fish is particularly important in helping to keep your arteries unclogged and your heart functioning healthily. If you've always been a meat-every-day-person try having fish once or twice a week — grilling a small fillet of plaice or sole with a few tomatoes and mushrooms or baking fish wrapped in foil with a few herbs, some lemon juice and a little yoghurt. The chances are you'll love it.

Cooking in retirement, in other words, as well as being enjoyable is good for you but there may be a few things you should watch out for.

Dentistry

If you have a plate, dentures or crowns it pays to guard against things like chewy toffee and less obvious things like blackberry seeds; and if you think this is self-evident, you should talk to my dentist who is sick of replacing my crowns.

Digestion

In general, the sort of cooking you do in retirement should be kinder on your digestive system than food from restaurants, canteens or the convenience shelves of supermarkets, but everybody's insides are different and one man's *poisson* can be another man's stomach ache. You'll notice that although we haven't included a lot of fried food there are none the less several fried dishes you might enjoy. If you have a medical condition which precludes fried food altogether then obviously you should leave it alone but if, on the other hand, fried food sometimes upsets your digestion but you fancy one of the recipes, try eating a very small amount and see what happens. Next time, if there have been no ill effects, you could eat a little more, but save the real Oliver Twist act for things you know you can eat without suffering afterwards.

The sort of foods you are cooking in retirement should help 'maintain regularity' or whatever is the current euphemism for keeping the bowels working — as they contain plenty of fibre. In fact, some vegetable soups, especially those made with dried pulses, should not be consumed before social occasions other than by those with the ability to assume expressions of total innocence.

Seriously, with regular meals, more fresh food and less stress, your digestive system should be fine but, if not, you could always try a bran breakfast cereal or the army's favourite − prunes − which are not called 'little blackcoated workers' for nothing. If you are still unhappy after a couple of days it could be worthwhile having a word with your doctor.

It's not too fanciful to maintain that the nearest thing to a perfect diet for our species was that of the hunter gatherer who lived on fresh fruit, fresh tubers, fresh nuts and occasional meat from animals that had been running so far and fast that there wasn't much fat left on them. In other words, it was a balanced diet and it is a balanced diet that we should aim for in retirement.

The move to lower fat/higher fibre meals can be accomplished without much difficulty. Add more vegetables and fruit − except the canned in heavy syrup variety − to your menus, include fish more often in your diet, avoid fatty meat and things like sausages on a regular basis, replace most of your butter and margarine by low fat spreads and margarines high in polyunsaturates and replace some of your white flour and white bread product by wholemeal and wholegrain ones.

With a little care you should soon strike a healthy balance, but if you are advised to follow a totally fat-free diet don't despair − you don't have to cut out all your favourite foods immediately. Follow the recipe for The Easiest Bread in the World (page 7) to make your own fat-free loaves and rolls. Fat-free pastry isn't difficult if you follow a few basic rules and you'll find recipes for both savoury and sweet pastry in the following pages. We've found, however, that wholemeal flour is not really satisfactory for fat-free cooking as it has a much heavier consistency but it's worth experimenting. Start off with white flour, next try using one eighth, then one quarter of wholemeal until you find the amount which suits you. We find we can use a little more wholemeal in savoury pastries with better results than in sweet dishes.

 # Basic Fat-free Pastry for Savoury Recipes

Imperial (Metric)

6 oz (175 g) self-raising flour
pinch salt
3 tablespoons low fat powdered
   skimmed milk*
water to mix

American

1½ cups self-rising flour
pinch salt
3 tablespoons low fat powdered
   skimmed milk*
water to mix

* You will find brands of milk with 0.15% fat only which is regarded as medically permissible.

1. Sieve all dry ingredients into a bowl. Mix to a stiff dough with a little water.
2. Roll out on a floured board.

This quantity is enough for 2 open tarts, 1 covered 8 inch (20 cm) plate pie or 1 lined and covered pudding basin (1½ pint) (850 ml).

Variations
1. Add 1 teaspoon mixed herbs when making vegetable pie.
2. Add dessertspoon finely chopped onion for meat or vegetable pudding.
3. Add 1½ dessertspoons sugar for Basic Fat-Free Sweet Pastry Recipe.

You can now make a wide vaiety of pies and tarts.

 # Chicken Pie

Preparation time: 20 minutes
Cooking time: 25 minutes

Imperial (Metric)
Filling
Pastry as above
¾ lb (350 g) chopped cooked chicken
4 oz (110 g) chopped mushrooms
small bunch spring onions, chopped
½ teaspoon mixed herbs
½ pint (275 ml) water
4 tablespoons powdered skimmed milk
salt and pepper

American
Filling
Pastry as above
1½ cups chopped cooked chicken
¼ lb chopped mushrooms
small bunch scallions, chopped
½ teaspoon mixed herbs
1⅓ cups water
4 tablespoons powdered skimmed milk
salt and pepper

1. Line 8 inch (20 cm) pie plate with half of pastry.
2. Mix water, skimmed milk, herbs, heat slowly − stirring continuously − until it thickens into a sauce. Add chicken, onions and mushrooms. Mix thoroughly and spread over pastry. Season and cover with remaining pastry. Cook at 400°F/200°C/Gas Mark 6 for 25 minutes. Serve with green beans and boiled new potatoes.

Variations
1. Replace chicken with cooked rabbit or turkey.
2. Replace herbs with 1 teaspoon curry powder.

Vegetable Cobbler

Preparation time: 20 minutes
Cooking time: 40 minutes

Imperial (Metric)

1 large potato
1 large onion
2 medium carrots
4 oz (110 g) mushrooms
½ pint (275 ml) stock
bay leaf
1 teaspoon mixed herbs
salt and pepper
½ basic pastry mix

American

1 large potato
1 large onion
2 medium carrots
¼ lb mushrooms
1⅓ cups stock
bay leaf
1 teaspoon mixed herbs
salt and pepper
½ basic pastry mix

1. Chop all vegetables and bring to boil with herbs and stock. Cook gently until tender − about 15 minutes.
2. Roll out pastry on floured board. Place cooked vegetables and stock in deep ovenproof dish. Remove bay leaf. Adjust seasoning if necessary. Cut pastry into 2 inch (5 cm) rounds and arrange on top of dish. Bake in oven (400°F/200°C/Gas Mark 6) for 25 minutes.

Variations

Replace vegetables with any others in season but keep the potato and either onion or leek. Experiment with seasonings. Add herbs to pastry cobbler.

Beef Roll

Preparation time: 30 minutes

Cooking time: 1½ to 2 hours depending on meat

Imperial (Metric)

¾ lb (350 g) lean beef (skirt)
1 large onion
salt and pepper
large potato
basic pastry mix
water

American

¾ lb lean stewing steak
1 large onion
salt and pepper
large potato
basic pastry mix
water

1. Trim any fat from meat and cut into small cubes. Chop onion and peel and cube potato. Bring to boil with enough water to cover, add seasoning and simmer until meat is tender.
2. Mix pastry, roll out into rectangle on floured board. Drain meat mixture, allow to cool and place on half of pastry, leaving a border. Damp border with cold water, fold over other half and press to seal. Use fork to crimp edges.
3. Bake at 400°F/200°C/Gas Mark 6 for about 20 minutes until golden brown.

Serve with mashed carrots and a green vegetable.

Variations
1. Replace beef with lean breast of chicken or boneless white fish. Adjust cooking time accordingly.
2. Replace filling by leeks and potato, 1 teaspoon mixed herbs. Simmer in vegetable stock until tender then proceed as above.

 # Apple Tart

Preparation time: 30 minutes
Cooking time: 30 minutes

Imperial (Metric)	**American**
1 lb (450 g) weight apples after peeling and coring	*1 lb weight apples after peeling and coring*
3 or 4 tablespoons granulated sugar	*3 or 4 tablespoons granulated sugar*
½ basic sweet pastry mix	*½ basic sweet pastry mix*

1. Roll out pastry on floured board and line 8 inch (20 cm) tart or flan dish. Prick pastry and bake blind for ten minutes (fill with rice paper and dried beans if necessary). Stew apples with sugar in a little water until almost soft but not broken.
2. Fill flan case, sprinkle a little sugar over top and bake at 425°F/220°C/Gas Mark 7 for about 20 minutes.

Variations
1. Try any other stewed fruits in season. Sugar depends on the fruit.
2. You can also use this sweet pastry for custards — made with egg or custard powder — or treacle tart — make the filling for this with ½ lb (225 g) (2 cups) soft breadcrumbs, 3 tablespoons syrup or molasses, finely grated peel of a lemon. Mix and fill pastry case after it has been baked blind for 10 minutes. Bake tart at 375°F/190°C/Gas Mark 5 for 25 minutes.

Sorbets and water ices as well as fresh fruit salads will also ring the changes.
Vegetable soups, thickened with lentils or other pulses, liquidised and well seasoned are useful fat-free dishes. It's a good idea to start a special recipe file and search out the most interesting ones instead of feeling deprived because butter, cheese and bacon are off the menu. Non-stick pans are particularly useful in fat-free cookery and, as it's not possible to grease baking tins, you should use rice paper or special parchment paper where necessary.
Don't fall into the trap of thinking that just because your diet is restricted it must be uninteresting. You'll find many recipes without fat in various cookery books and, if you have to cut down on sugar as well, there are satisfactory substitutes nowadays which you can use in most dishes. It takes a little time to find one that's just right for you but it's worth the effort. After all, if a balanced diet improves your health you'll enjoy cooking — and eating — in retirement so much more.

Try to use herbs more adventurously — a little fennel with puréed carrots, for instance, will compensate for the lack of butter.

Fresh fruits set in jelly make attractive fat-free desserts, and there are endless variations from the simple grated apple in raspberry jelly to melons filled with grapes set in jelly which are attractive enough for party fare.

You can still enjoy scones spread with honey or strawberry jam even though you are on a fat-free diet and you can also adapt this recipe for a savoury scone.

 ## Scones

Preparation time: 10 minutes

Cooking time: 15 minutes

Imperial (Metric)	American
4 oz (110 g) self-raising flour	*1 cup self-rising flour*
2 level tablespoons powdered skimmed milk	*2 level tablespoons powdered skimmed milk*
½ level tablespoon (10 g) caster sugar	*½ level tablespoon caster sugar*
1 egg white	*1 egg white*
pinch of cream of tartar	*pinch cream of tartar*
2 tablespoons (50 g) raisins (optional)	*2 tablespoons raisins (optional)*
pinch of salt	*pinch of salt*

1. Mix dry ingredients in a bowl. Whisk egg white and then stir it into the mixture, together with raisins if used. Add a little milk made up from powder to get a soft dough.

2. Roll out on floured board to ½ inch (1 cm) thickness. Mark top with a cross so that it will later divide into four sections and place on a non-stick baking sheet.

3. Bake at 450°F/230°C/Gas Mark 8 for about 15 minutes. Spread with jam or honey and eat while still warm.

For a savoury scone, omit sugar and raisins and replace by a pinch of dried oregano, basil or chopped parsley. Spread with Bovril or Marmite and eat while still warm.

(Facing) **Picnic:** Scotch Eggs, Leek and Cheese Puffs, Mushroom and Courgette Loaf, Sesame Chick Peas, Chicken Drumsticks, Chinese Leaf Salad, Avocado Pâté, Garlic Butter, Parsley Butter, Fruit Kebabs, Melon filled with Grapes in Jelly, Blackberry Curd Pudding

9

People in Retirement

Cooking for Two

Our friend Ted has been happily retired for twenty years, so he and his wife Dorothy seemed obvious people to talk to about cooking in retirement.

Ted is an 84-year-old Yorkshireman who started work as an apprentice blacksmith in the coal mines on his thirteenth birthday. He and Dorothy moved south in 1956 to be nearer their son and Ted retired from his job as storeman for the Bristol Aircraft Corporation in 1967.

Dorothy too left school at thirteen to look after her invalid mother, three older brothers and a younger sister before starting work as a bookbinder at fifteen.

Ted and Dorothy live on the State Pension, rent rebate and a small pension from BAC and, while they are far from wealthy, they enjoy a life style which many people would envy, largely because they seem to have got everything about living and cooking in retirement absolutely right.

'Since I've been retired,' Ted told me, 'I often wonder how I ever found the time to go to work. Being able to go to my allotment whenever I want to has made a tremendous difference. I can go every day if the weather is half way decent, which means I have time to do things properly and can grow a lot more food.'

Ted has a little over three hundred square yards of land which he rents from the city for just over £11 per year, including an elderly but serviceable garden hut. Slightly larger plots with new huts are a few pounds more.

'It's a biggish plot and I can grow almost all our vegetables, salad stuffs and soft fruit for the whole year,' said Ted, 'including plenty to swap or give to friends and family.

'Of course gardening and cooking take time but now we have all the time we need and we certainly enjoy our food.'

Dorothy, who is also in her eighties, has cooked and baked for a family since she left school and, for her, retirement has made a considerable difference by turning cooking into what she calls 'a joint job'.

Said Dorothy, 'When you come to think of it there's hardly anything we do alone; there's always one part that Ted does and another that I do. It's always

(Facing) **Feeding the Five Thousand Cheaply:** Left: ingredients from which all food shown on right was made. Right Clockwise: Onion Rings, Apple Rings, Mushroom Puffs, Potato Beignets. Sauce: top of the milk shaken in an almost empty tomato sauce bottle

been a joint affair since he retired. I never start to bake without him and he wouldn't think of starting without me.

'When we bake bread I do the mixing and Ted does the kneading, although nowadays he uses the food processor which is a great help.

'Ted always prepares the vegetables and I cook them. We never get in each other's way because we've done it so often we know exactly what to do next and as soon as I've finished one lot of cooking, for example, Ted will be clearing up and getting ready for the next.

'We save a lot of money by growing so much of our own food and cooking everything fresh but I've never worked out how much. I watch people buying "convenience" foods in the shops and wonder how on earth they can afford it.

'We never buy bread, cakes or pies but I do like biscuits, especially chocolate ones, and we do buy those.

'We don't have a cooked breakfast nowadays — although we always had one, usually eggs and bacon, when Ted was working and went on doing it for years out of force of habit.

'Nowadays we just have cereal, toast and marmalade — home-made of course — that sort of thing.

'We always have our main meal at mid-day because it suits us better. When Ted was working we had to have our big meal when he came home at night but that wasn't from choice — it was from necessity.

'Retirement has changed all that. It enables us to eat when we want to eat; in fact, we've been able to do pretty nearly everything when we wanted to do it.

'Cooking when you want to cook, rather than when you have to is one of the special joys of retirement.

'We find the small freezer compartment extremely useful and of course we make all our own jams and marmalades. In a good year we freeze so much that we have our own blackcurrants — our favourites — all year round.

'We have very good food and we both enjoy it. In fact, eating is one of our main pleasures which makes cooking very important, especially as our two grandsons love our old-fashioned traditional dishes. For instance, we always have hotpot once a week and although I make it on different days they often seem to know when I'm going to make it and arrive just in time.'

 ## Dorothy's Hot Pot (for two people)

Preparation time: 20 minutes
Cooking time: 2 hours approximately

Imperial (Metric)	**American**
1 lamb chop per person	*1 lamb chop per person*
2 large potatoes	*2 large potatoes*
1 large onion	*1 large onion*
2 carrots	*2 carrots*
tablespoon sugar	*tablespoon sugar*
1 apple	*1 apple*
salt and pepper	*salt and pepper*
bouquet garni	*bouquet garni*
tablespoon of butter or lard for frying	*tablespoon of butter or lard for frying*

Fry lamb chops to seal, and lightly fry chopped onion. Place a layer of sliced potato in the bottom of a large enamel casserole — this is what Dorothy always uses but you could substitute any large ovenproof dish — cover with a layer of onion, then the lamb chops, then a layer of thinly sliced carrot, seasoning and the apple chopped small. Cover with a second layer of potatoes and add enough water with bouquet garni to cover. Dorothy likes to add some gravy to the liquid then cook for two hours in a slow oven (300°F/150°C/Gas Mark 2).

 ## Dorothy's Bread

Preparation time: about 1 hour
Cooking time: large loaf 45 minutes, small loaf 30 minutes,
rolls 15 minutes

Imperial (Metric)

1½ lb (700 g) strong white flour
2 teaspoons salt
½ oz (10 g) fresh yeast or 3 level
*   teaspoons dried yeast*
2 oz (50 g) margarine
14 fl oz (400 ml) water
teaspoon sugar

American

6 cups white flour
2 teaspoons salt
3 level teaspoons dried yeast
4 level tablespoons margarine
1½ cups water
teaspoon sugar

1. Mix yeast with a little warm water and sugar in jug, stir then add rest of water and leave to froth — usually about ten minutes in a warm place.
2. Mix flour and salt together, then rub in fat. Make a hollow in the centre and mix in the yeast water gradually.
3. Knead the bread until you have a smooth elastic dough that comes cleanly from the bowl. By hand this takes about ten minutes. Cover the bowl with a cloth and leave in a warm place to rise. Knead again briefly and divide into bread tins, pressing down in the tins. Cover and leave to rise to the top of the tins. This usually takes about 30 minutes. Alternatively divide into small rolls. At 425°F/220°C/Gas Mark 7 a large loaf takes 45 minutes, small loaves take 30 minutes and rolls take 15.

To make a brown loaf Dorothy uses 1 lb (450 g) (4 cups) wholemeal (whole wheat flour) and ½ lb (225 g) (2 cups) strong white.

'As a thrifty Yorkshirewoman,' says Dorothy, 'I don't like to see money wasted so I always arrange to make two or three dishes that will go in the oven together so that if I'm making, say, hotpot, I'll make a rice pudding or a chocolate cake at the same time.

'Another little economy is that when I mix the ingredients for bread I often make extra and put it in the freezer. Of course it always helps to be able to exchange things we've grown − Ted grows so many strawberries, for example, that we have loads to give away and other people with gardens and allotments are equally generous with their gooseberries and so on.'

 # Dorothy's Gooseberry and Apple Pie

This recipe is adaptable to any size dish. Simply line with shortcrust pastry and fill shallow ovenproof dish with pastry. Beat up 1 egg with 2 dessertspoons sugar. Bring ¼ pint (150 ml) (just over ½ cup) milk to the boil the pour it onto the beaten egg. Put pastry case in oven for about 10 minutes to bake partly. Remove can be popped in the oven whenever there is room.

 # Dorothy's Egg Custard Tart

This is a good oven filler when you have a little shortcrust left over. Line a small shallow ovenproof dish with pastry. Beat up 1 egg with 2 dessertspoons sugar. Bring ¼ pint (150 ml) (just over ½ cup) milk to the boil then pour it onto the beaten egg. Put pastry case in oven for about ten minutes to bake partly. Remove and pour egg mixture in. Sprinkle with nutmeg and return to oven (350°F/180°C/ Gas Mark 4) for about 15 minutes or until set.

 # Dorothy's Special Chocolate Cake

Preparation time: 20 minutes
Cooking time: 45−50 minutes

This can go in the oven at the same time as the egg custard.

Imperial (Metric)

6 oz (175 g) self-raising flour
4 oz (110 g) butter or margarine
4 oz (110 g) sugar
2 eggs, beaten

American

1½ cups self-rising flour
½ cup butter or margarine
½ cup sugar
2 eggs, beaten

4 oz (110 g) plain chocolate, grated *¼ lb plain chocolate, grated*
1 oz (25 g) chopped nuts *2 tablespoons chopped nuts*

1. Beat butter and sugar until creamy then add beaten eggs and flour. Mix in 2 oz (50 g) (half) grated chocolate and 2 tablespoons water. Beat well.
2. Line a loose-bottomed cake tin with greaseproof paper, spoon in mixture and bake at 350°F/180°C/Gas Mark 4 for 45−50 minutes.
3. Remove from tin when cool. Melt remainder of chocolate in a basin over hot water and spread over top of cake.

One of Dorothy's favourites, which she makes regularly during the soft fruit season, is Summer Pudding. This varies according to the fruit available but blackcurrants are probably first choice.

 # Dorothy's Summer Pudding

Line a buttered basin with slices of bread − remove crusts first − until the bottom and sides are completely covered. Stew blackcurrants and sugar to taste until cooked. Then simply fill the basin with fruit and cover with a layer of bread. Put a small plate or saucer on top to fit inside the basin, put a heavy weight on − 2lb jar of jam is about right − and leave overnight. Turn out next day. Utterly delicious on its own or served with cream or ice cream.

Cooking in retirement enables Ted and Dorothy to save money but, more importantly, it allows them to be generous and hospitable with their friends and family. Not that they wouldn't always be welcome just for themselves, of course, but it's great to turn up laden with a basket of strawberries or some pots of splendid home-made jam from fruit picked that morning and to see the pleasure on someone's face as you hand them over.

Cooking for One

Jenny, who is 67, was the senior secretary of a School of Fashion and it shows in the stylish clothes she designs and makes for her own wardrobe. Her son Richard is a lecturer in musicology and lives away from home so most days since her retirement, seven years ago, she has been cooking for herself.

'You don't cook the same things for one person as you do for several,' she told me. 'You tend to keep it fairly simple − at least I do.

'I've never had a cooked breakfast so making do with a plate of muesli or grapefruit and a cup of coffee now that I've retired is from choice.

'I sometimes cook a traditional Sunday lunch − although not very often − but usually at lunchtime I have something light like cheese on toast or a sandwich, with perhaps a little fresh fruit to finish.

'At about four o'clock − if I'm at home − I have a cup of tea with a piece of cake or a biscuit and then cook my main meal of the day for about six thirty. Eating at precisely the same time every day is a little old-making so although I do have a routine I occasionally break it by having my main meal at lunchtime which, as you get older, is probably better for the digestion anyway.

'One temptation I don't succumb to is to go without cooking altogether. I have a step-sister who says that when her family is away she just eats something while standing at the kitchen sink but for someone living alone that sort of thing could create a dangerous precedent.

'Shopping for one person can be difficult but, although I usually avoid the very big shops, I find most shop people are helpful if you explain that you only want enough for one.

'I know someone in the same position as myself who buys an enormous roast every week for Sunday lunch and is still eating it on Wednesday when she throws half of it away because she's bored with it.

'I buy just one chop or perhaps half a pound of minced [ground] beef which makes a Shepherd's Pie on one day and Chilli con Carne the day after. I find those small cartons of dried mixed peppers very useful because I can use just a spoonful whereas I would waste most of a fresh pepper.

'Normally — although I always have a dessert — I like to keep things simple but sometimes if I'm a bit bored I'll make myself, say, a meringue sweet — just for the Hell of it — or I might think "Gosh, I haven't had a fruit pie for ages" and decide to make some pastry.'

With only herself to please Jenny has discovered the usefulness of a fixed routine — and the joy of breaking it — together with the pleasure of interspersing her everyday fare with the occasional gourmet meal for one.

This can sometimes be tricky. 'Most recipes in gourmet cook books are for four to six people and you have to do some complicated figuring to get them down to one portion but, while a lot of people wouldn't take the trouble, I consider that now I'm retired I have the time to spare — so why not?'

Since she stopped work Jenny has discovered one or two ways in which she can make cooking easier. For instance, when she is making a pie she also bakes several small empty shells 'blind' and uses them later with either sweet or savoury fillings.

'One thing you don't make for one person is a big steamed pudding – and I love them although they are ruinous for one's figure. So, if I'm making a batch of cakes I often make a pudding mixture and fill some little castle pudding tins. They take only about fifteen minutes to steam and I warm them up at a later date and have them with custard or cream. Talking of cream, when I'm on my own I usually substitute yoghurt because of the calories but guests usually get real cream. I also like to keep in a packet of something like Dream Topping — a cream powder which you mix with milk — I find it useful because I can mix just a spoonful whenever I want without any waste.'

Here are some of Jenny's recipes.

 # Jenny's Curried Fish (for one)

Preparation time: 5 minutes
Cooking time: 20 minutes

Imperial (Metric)

4 oz (110 g) white fish
½ oz (10 g) butter

American

4 oz white fish
1 tablespoon butter

heaped teaspoon plain flour	*heaped teaspoon all purpose flour*
½ teaspoon curry powder	*½ teaspoon curry powder*

Make a roux with butter, flour and curry powder. Spread the roux over the piece of fish. Bake at 400°F/200°C/Gas Mark 6 for 20 minutes in a shallow ovenproof dish.

Serve with green vegetables.

Jenny usually bakes a second piece of fish at the same time to save fuel. This one is simply dotted with butter and cooked for the same length of time. She uses it next day in the following recipe.

Jenny's Savoury Fish Dish (for one)

Preparation time: 10 minutes
Cooking time: 10 minutes

Imperial (Metric)

4 oz (110 g) cooked white fish
¼ pint (150 ml) thick white sauce
2 tablespoons grated cheese
1 tablespoon soft white breadcrumbs
salt and pepper

American

4 oz cooked white fish
just over ½ cup thick white sauce
2 tablespoons grated cheese
1 tablespoon soft white breadcrumbs
salt and pepper

Flake fish into a small pan containing thick white sauce. Heat gently for 5 minutes then turn onto heatproof plate, season, sprinkle with breadcrumbs and grated cheese and brown under grill.

Serve with vegetables for a main meal or with toast triangles for a snack.

Scandinavian Fish (for one)

Preparation time: 10 minutes
Cooking time: 10 minutes

Imperial (Metric)

4 oz (110 g) boneless white fish
1 medium onion
vegetable oil
a little flour seasoned with salt and
  pepper

American

4 oz boneless white fish
1 medium onion
vegetable oil
a little flour seasoned with salt and
  pepper

1. Cut fish into small squares, roll in seasoned flour and fry in shallow oil until cooked and brown. Keep hot while you fry finely chopped onion.
2. Serve fish with browned onions on top.

Jenny's Quick Chilli con Carne

Preparation time: 5 minutes
Cooking time: 20 minutes

Imperial (Metric)

4 oz (110 g) minced beef
1 small onion
¼ pint (150 ml) stock
¼ teaspoon chilli powder
teaspoon dried red and green peppers
½ small tin baked beans
salt and pepper

American

4 oz ground beef
1 small onion
just over ½ cup stock
¼ teaspoon chilli powder
teaspoon dried red and green peppers
½ small tin baked beans
salt and pepper

1. Fry minced beef and finely chopped onion for five minutes, then add stock, peppers and seasoning. Simmer for 10 minutes.
2. Add beans and cook for a further 5 minutes.

 # Tomato Snack

Preparation time: 5 minutes
Cooking time: 5 minutes

Imperial (Metric)

2 medium tomatoes
small onion
heaped teaspoon brown sugar
large pinch curry powder
pinch salt

American

2 medium tomatoes
small onion
heaped teaspoon brown sugar
large pinch curry powder
pinch salt

1. Cut tomatoes in half. Mix finely chopped onion with sugar and seasonings.
2. Pile mixture on tomatoes and grill for 5 minutes.
3. Serve on hot buttered toast.

 # Gypsy Jacket Potato

Preparation time: 5 minutes
Cooking time: about 1½ hours depending on size of potato

Imperial (Metric)

1 large potato

American

1 large potato

2 tablespoons grated cheese
¼ teaspoon dried sage or teaspoon
   fresh chopped
2 thin slices of apple

2 tablespoons grated cheese
½ teaspoon dried sage or teaspoon
   fresh chopped
2 thin slices of apple

1. Bake potato. Cut in two and scoop out insides. Mash with grated cheese and sage.
2. Pile mixture into potato skins. Top each half with a slice of apple and return to oven until the apple is soft.

Jenny entertains frequently and her guests include former colleagues — many of whom are now also retired — and people she has met since her retirement. She is an active member of various organisations and maintains a keen interest in the theatre and music.

'When I have people for a meal I like to keep the main dish simple — something like a casserole so that it doesn't matter if people are late — and let myself go on the starters and desserts which can be prepared in advance.

'I learned the hard way that when you are on your own entertaining means being cook, butler, barman, cloakroom attendant, hostess — the lot — so it pays to keep things simple. Find out your guests' preferences by all means but don't give them a multiple choice. Don't ask people what they would like to drink or you'll be mixing individual drinks all evening. Ask them if they'd like dry sherry or medium, and white wine or red.'

Jenny has found out one way in which retired people can give their guests pleasure without it costing a penny. 'I refuse to accept help with the washing up because many of my guests have husbands and children and it makes a real treat for them not to have to worry about the dishes.'

At 67 Jenny still has the outlook of a much younger woman and plans keeping things that way, but Ted and Dorothy, although remarkably fit and healthy for their mid-eighties, are already making one or two concessions to age. They found it increasingly difficult some time ago, for instance, to knead dough and, though they resisted at first, finally accepted a food mixer as a Diamond Wedding gift.

Kate is older still and is now getting a bit frail although only a few years ago, when asked by a health visitor whether she would consider 'Meals on Wheels' she replied that she would be glad to help and how many days did they need her.

She still cooks for herself but no longer lugs around huge pans of boiling soup — something many younger people should avoid if possible. In fact, with the help of her family, she has gone out of her way to make her cooking easier and safer. The kitchen of her modern bungalow, for example, has a non-slip floor and lever handles have replaced the door knobs which she could no longer manage because of her poor grip. Her kitchen fitments have been adapted to include pull-out wire baskets and carousel units incorporated into slightly lower than average base units and her shallow sink has a lever mix tap with an extended handle.

A lightweight trolley copes with things she used to carry and she uses it more and more, pushing it through the swing door from her kitchen to her combined dining and sitting room.

She gives visitors heart failure by making frequent use of her two step aluminium folding ladder but tells everyone what an improvement it is on the kitchen chairs she used to use.

For some time now she has been collecting specially designed small kitchen equipment usually for Christmas and birthday presents so that in addition to the normal things like electric can opener, small mixer and so on, she now has a selection of gadgets like gripping aids and mixing bowl holders and a special bread board which, like her meat carving dish, is fitted with short spikes at one end to prevent the bread from slipping.

Other useful devices include openers for screw top bottles and jars, wine bottles, ring cans and cartons and special pads to prevent plates, bowls, chopping boards and so on from slipping.

Her polypropylene electric kettle has an automatic cut-out and is lighter than most metal ones and the family have tested out her pans — surreptitiously — to make sure that they are stable and not inclined to tip over on her cooker.

Kate would firmly reject any suggestion that she is 'handicapped' but old age is itself a handicap which — with luck — will come to us all and it's as well there are these sort of gadgets to help us cope.

As far as cooking is concerned Kate's life style as a widow of long standing with an income sufficient for her needs is similar to Jenny's except that she likes to make a lot of cakes which makes her popular with her grandchildren. This ensures that they drop in frequently, which is in itself a built-in security device as she feels that she must always have enough food in the house to feed a regiment while they in turn make sure she eats enough of her own cooking — and a few specialities they bring — to keep healthy.

Kate is fortunate in her family who live near enough to help her make marmalade and jams from the fruit in her garden and help her with the garden itself — a job which she enjoys but finds impossible to tackle alone. And she's fortunate too that, apart from not being quite as strong as she was and becoming just a mite forgetful, she has no other handicaps.

For those retired people with serious disabilities or handicaps there is help to be had from organisations like the Disabled Living Foundation at 380/384 Harrow Road, London, who can supply lists of household fittings and equipment specially designed for those with mobility or sensory problems. Information can also be obtained in the UK and many other countries from the utility companies and from the larger manufacturers of fitted kitchens.

Luckily for Tom and Laura, unless either of them sprains a wrist on the golf course or squash court, it should be a long time before they have to worry about any sort of handicap other than the sporting variety.

Mind you, Tom and Laura are atypical as they are both under sixty-five and, as a former insurance broker and paediatrician respectively, have a combined retirement income which would make most people's pre-retirement one look sick.

Atypically, too, with the exception of soft fruit, they have now stopped gardening for the pot and turned their largish suburban garden over to lawns and flowers with a wide paved area for eating outside and summer entertaining.

Now that their children are all grown up and living abroad Laura says she cooks less than before, although this is also partly for reasons of diet because both she and Tom have a tendency to put on weight.

'When we eat alone I do very simple things but always with the best ingredients and although we don't diet as such we tend to eat the things we know are good for us like fish and fresh fruit and avoid the heavier fatty foods.

'It's really quite pleasant to know that we have no one to bother about but ourselves for meals most of the time.

'I've always enjoyed cooking and now that I have more time I find that when we entertain I like to make at least one elaborate dish — my desserts are often rather spectacular concoctions that take ages to prepare but that's what I enjoy doing. When I was working and running a home there simply wasn't the time to make the sort of things that are now my speciality.

'Tom looks after the drinks; he has always bought good wine but since he retired he's been going to tastings and learning more about the subject so that even though he only spends about the same − or even less − the wines he chooses are better and he also manages to pick up the odd bargain at the supermarket, simply by knowing what to look for.

'He has even started helping in the kitchen − something he never did before we retired − which makes cooking more fun for me. He clears up, fills the dishwasher, that sort of thing, and sometimes lends a hand with gourmet dishes, especially if the recipe has wine in it. However, apart from barbecues, where he takes over completely, he won't do any of the day to day cooking and I've yet to get him to peel a potato.'

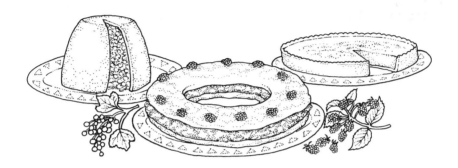

 ## Laura's Raspberry Ring

Preparation time: about 40 minutes
Cooking time: 35 minutes

Laura often uses choux pastry for her desserts and finds that a ring or crown of pastry can be used for many recipes. This is one that her guests particularly appreciate.

Imperial (Metric)

Choux pastry
2½ oz (65 g) plain flour
2 oz (50 g) butter
salt
2 eggs
¼ pint (150 ml) water

American

Choux pastry
2 heaped, 1 level tablespoon all purpose
* flour*
¼ cup butter
salt
2 eggs
just over ½ cup water

1. Bring water and butter to boil in small saucepan, stirring until butter has melted.
2. Remove from heat and pour over bowl of sifted flour and salt. Beat until it comes away cleanly from the sides of the bowl. A wooden spoon is usually best for this.
3. Beat in eggs one at a time, using electric mixer if possible, until mixture is completely smooth. Pipe onto a greased and floured baking tray in a ring 8 inch (20 cm) diameter. Bake at 400°F/200°C/Gas Mark 6 for about 25 minutes or until risen and crisp. Remove from oven and with a very sharp knife slit in half horizontally and leave two halves to cool.

Filling

1 lb (450 g) raspberries (fresh or frozen)	1 lb raspberries (fresh or frozen)
2 tablespoons caster sugar	2 tablespoons caster sugar
1/2 pint (275 ml) double cream	1 1/3 cups heavy cream
icing sugar	confectioner's sugar

1. Blend raspberries with sugar until smooth then pass through fine sieve to remove any seeds. Whisk cream until thick and fold into raspberry purée.
2. Before serving, carefully spoon mixture into the bottom of the choux ring and place the top on neatly. Sprinkle with a little icing sugar (confectioner's sugar) – you can make this, by the way, by blending caster sugar for about 30 seconds. Place any remaining purée in the centre of the ring and decorate with a few fresh raspberries dipped in icing sugar.

Variations
Strawberries or gooseberries are both excellent alternatives.

Chocolate filling

Imperial (Metric)	American
1/2 lb (225 g) ginger biscuits	1/2 lb ginger biscuits
4 oz (110 g) chopped walnuts	1 cup chopped walnuts
2 tablespoons caster sugar	2 tablespoons caster sugar
2 tablespoons butter	2 tablespoons butter
4 oz (110 g) grated dark chocolate	1/4 lb grated dark chocolate
1/2 pint (275 ml) double cream	1 1/3 cups heavy cream

1. Grind biscuits, walnuts and caster sugar until fine.
2. Melt butter and add to biscuit mixture. Stir in. Melt chocolate in a bowl over hot water and add to biscuit mixture, stirring until smoothly blended. Whip cream until stiff and fold into biscuit mixture. Proceed as for raspberry ring.

This is a very rich dessert and will serve more guests than the raspberry ring. The chocolate filling can also be used to fill meringues or cakes or can be served by itself as a rich chocolate dessert, perhaps with fantail biscuits.

The recipe for choux pastry can be used for choux puffs which can be filled individually or assembled in a 'mountain' with cream filling and chocolate sauce.

 # Laura's Orange Shortbread Pudding

Preparation time: 25 minutes
Cooking time: 1 hour 35 minutes

Shortbread base

Imperial (Metric)	American
6 oz (175 g) plain flour	1 1/2 cups all purpose flour
1 heaped tablespoon caster sugar	1 heaped tablespoon caster sugar
finely grated rind of orange	finely grated rind of orange
4 oz (110 g) butter	1/2 cup butter

Butter a 9 inch (23 cm) flan dish. Sift flour and sugar into a bowl. Work in butter and rind with floured hands until it forms a sticky dough. Press down evenly into flan dish, prick with fork and bake for 20 minutes at 400°F/200°C/Gas Mark 6. Leave to cool.

Orange topping

Imperial (Metric)	American
grated rind of 2 oranges	*grated rind of 2 oranges*
juice of 3 oranges	*juice of 3 oranges*
4 eggs	*4 eggs*
2 tablespoons Cointreau (optional)	*2 tablespoons Cointreau (optional)*
2 oz (50 g) caster sugar	*2 level tablespoons caster sugar*

1. Put the yolks in a double boiler, add the sugar and the orange juice gradually, stirring all the time. Keep water at simmering until the custard mixture thickens. Add grated rind and liqueur. Leave to cool.
2. Whisk egg whites until stiff, fold into the cooled orange custard and pile on the biscuit base. Bake at 300°F/150°/Gas Mark 2 until golden brown – about 60 minutes. Serve at once.

For a particularly special occasion Laura serves this dessert with cream whipped with a tablespoon of Cointreau.

Variation
Replace orange with lemons or limes but double the sugar and substitute rum for the Cointreau.

 # Laura's Macaroons with Almond Cream

For this recipe it's a good idea to make the macaroons in advance. They freeze well or keep well in a tight-lidded biscuit tin.

Preparation time: 30 minutes
Cooking time: 25 minutes

Macaroons

Imperial (Metric)	American
6 oz (175 g) caster sugar	*¾ cup caster sugar*
4 oz (110 g) ground almonds	*1 cup ground almonds*
2 egg whites	*2 egg whites*
3 drops almond essence	*3 drops almond essence*
few flaked almonds	*few flaked almonds*

Whisk egg whites until they peak. Stir in the sugar and whisk again. Add the rest of the ingredients and stir to a stiff mix. Take small spoonsful, roll into a ball and press onto rice paper on a baking sheet. Place wide apart. Bake at 375°F/190°C/Gas Mark 5 for 15 minutes until lightly brown. Leave to cool before removing from baking tray.

Almond Cream

Imperial (Metric)	American
4 oz (110 g) ground almonds	*1 cup ground almonds*
½ pint (275 ml) double cream	*1⅓ cups heavy cream*
3 eggs, separated	*3 eggs, separated*
2 tablespoons flaked almonds	*2 tablespoons flaked almonds*
3 heaped tablespoons sugar	*3 heaped tablespoons sugar*
rind of an orange cut in strips	*rind of an orange cut in strips*
2 tablespoons water	*2 tablespoons water*

1. Place ground almonds, egg yolks, cream and 2 tablespoons sugar in top of double boiler. Stir constantly over low heat — on no account allow the mixture to boil or it will curdle — stir until it thickens to a custard-like consistency. Remove from heat and leave to cool.

2. Whip egg whites until very stiff. Fold into cooled custard and pile into separate serving dishes. Decorate with flaked almonds and chill.

3. Put water and 1 tablespoon sugar in thick based pan. Heat and stir until it caramelises. Add orange rind cut into very thin strips. Stir constantly until thickly coated and brittle. Remove carefully — they are very hot — and drain on wire grid over kitchen paper. When cold break up and scatter over top of desserts. Serve the desserts with a plate of macaroons.

10

The Sweets of Retirement

When most of us were kids a 'Saturday sixpence' would set us up in sweets for the week but nowadays children need to be independently wealthy to afford a chocolate bar and a sweet tooth in the family can seriously damage your bank balance.

Of course some of the horrendous price rises that leave Grandad looking like Munchausen or Billy Liar when he tries to tell the kids how much he could buy for a penny are due to increases in the cost of ingredients like sugar and chocolate and can't be avoided by even the most cunning do-it-yourself confectioner. However, a huge proportion of the increase is due to rises in the cost of labour, advertising, packaging and transport, not to mention items like administration, taxes and machinery, none of which significantly affects those of us who are cooking in retirement.

There is a tremendous variety of sweets one can make at home, ranging from the simplest of old fashioned toffees, which can be made in minutes for next to nothing, to expensive looking candies which take a little more time but can still be produced at a fraction of the cost you would have to pay in a shop. You also have the satisfaction of knowing that you have used good ingredients.

Most of us who grew up in Europe during World War II can remember the days when sweets and chocolates were either rationed or completely unobtainable. In England the ration was a couple of ounces a week and one of my most vivid memories is of my younger sister saving her ration until the rest of us had eaten ours in order to gloat over every mouth-watering morsel.

War-time sweets were simple and even when rationing ceased and ingredients became available, most home-made sweets remained uncomplicated. They still provide the basis for some splendid old-fashioned standbys for one's own consumption or for when the family call around.

Old-fashioned Sweets, Fudges and Mints

Anyone who can boil water can make toffee — in fact it's child's play and if you have grandchildren or young neighbours you could have plenty of willing 'helpers' whenever you are making it. One point to remember, however, if you do allow children in the kitchen is that toffee gets exceptionally hot. It's dangerous stuff if it boils over or spills and very young children should be kept away from it. Instead they could be kept safely occupied by rolling and cutting out fondant for peppermint creams and so on, and they could make sweets such as Marzipan Brazils which are simply small circles of marzipan carefully wrapped round brazil nuts. Crimped at the join and dusted with icing sugar they look very professional and children will enjoy making them as a present.

Older toffee makers who, like me, have caps or crowns should bear in mind that they can be endangered by over-enthusiastic chewing.

The only other danger involved in sweet making is a dietary one and it makes sense to go easy on the home-made goodies because their calorie content is high. It is a real temptation and when we were making the sweets for the illustration we scoffed a lot more than we intended, but we also were able to give a lot away.

 Bonfire Treacle Toffee

Preparation time: 5 minutes
Cooking time: about 30 minutes

This is Molly's mother's family recipe. She always made trays of it to be eaten on Bonfire Night together with baked potatoes and black peas. It's very quickly made and is so good that we make it several times a year. It keeps well in a tin — we put greaseproof paper between each layer — and is very soothing for a sore throat.

Imperial (Metric)	**American**
1 lb (450 g) brown sugar	*2½ cups soft brown sugar*
½ lb (225 g) black treacle	*½ cup black treacle or molasses*
4 oz (110 g) butter	*½ cup butter*
½ pint (275 ml) water	*1⅓ cups water*

1. Boil sugar, treacle and water for 20 minutes, then add butter and continue boiling and occasionally stirring until brittle stage. This is when a small spoonful dropped into cold water forms brittle strands.

Pour into greased shallow tin and leave till cold. Break into pieces when required and store in a jar or tin with tight fitting lid.

(Facing) **Afternoon Tea:** Double cake stand, top plate Potato Cakes, bottom plate Raisin Tea Bread. Clockwise: Orange Tea Bread, Fruit and Nut Loaf, Nut Crunch, Scones with Raspberry jam and clotted cream. Centre: Gingerbread

 # Brittle Toffee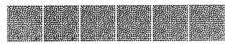

Preparation time: 5 minutes
Cooking time: about 30 minutes

This is a different family version — also called Bonfire Toffee but without treacle.

Imperial (Metric)

12 oz (350 g) soft brown sugar
2 oz (50 g) butter
1 tablespoon vinegar
2 tablespoons boiling water
pinch salt

American

just under 2 cups soft brown sugar
1/4 cup butter
1 tablespoon vingar
2 tablespoons boiling water
pinch salt

1. Bring all ingredients to boil and continue boiling until brittle thread stage.
2. Pour into shallow greased tin 8 in x 14 in (20 cm x 35 cm) and mark into squares before it is completely cold. Store in jar or tin.

 # Grandma's Chocolate Tablet

Preparation time: 10 minutes
Cooking time: about 20 minutes

This Scottish recipe has a very rich taste. It keeps well and makes an attractive gift.

Imperial (Metric)

1 lb (450 g) granulated sugar
2 oz (50 g) butter
1 oz (25 g) dark chocolate
1 tablespoon golden syrup
1/2 teaspoon vanilla essence
1 teaspoon sherry
1/4 pint (150 ml) milk

American

2 cups granulated sugar
1/4 cup butter
1 oz semi-sweet dark chocolate
1 tablespoon maple syrup
1/2 teaspoon vanilla essence
1 teaspoon sherry
just over 1/2 cup milk

1. Dissolve sugar, milk and syrup gently in a heavy bottomed pan. Add grated chocolate and stir until boiling. Cook to soft ball stage (when dropped in cold water) then take off heat and stir in butter.
2. Allow to cool slightly then beat in vanilla and sherry. Heat gently for one minute then beat until thick and opaque.
3. Pour into buttered tin and leave until absolutely cold before cutting into neat squares.

(Facing) **Dinner Party — Menu 1:** Seafood Pancakes, Parsley Butter, Tomato Sauce; Lemon Chicken, Vegetable Platter; Frozen Oranges

Barcelona Toffee

Preparation time: 5 minutes
Cooking time: about 30 minutes

Imperial (Metric)

1 lb (450 g) granulated sugar
1 oz (25 g) butter
1 dessertspoon vinegar
2 oz (50 g) chopped raisins
2 oz shelled almonds
1 teaspoon vanilla essence
1/2 pint (275 ml) water

American

2 cups granulated sugar
2 level tablespoons butter
1 dessertspoon vinegar
4 tablespoons chopped raisins
4 tablespoons shelled almonds
1 teaspoon vanilla essence
1 1/3 cups water

Put everything except nuts and vanilla into a heavy pan and boil to brittle stage.
Stir in nuts and vanilla and pour into greased tin. When cold break into pieces.

 # Old-fashioned Milk Toffee

Preparation time: 5 minutes
Cooking time: about 15 minutes

This recipe came from one of Molly's great aunts. Visiting children were given a
piece only if they were well behaved.

Imperial (Metric)

4 oz (110 g) butter
1 lb (450 g) soft brown sugar
small can condensed milk
6 drops vanilla essence

American

1/2 cup butter
2 1/2 cups soft brown sugar
small can condensed milk
6 drops vanilla essence

1. Melt butter in a heavy saucepan and when it bubbles start to add sugar, stirring
all the time with a wooden spoon. Cook for five minutes.
2. Add condensed milk, bring to boil quickly and boil for five minutes.
3. Remove from heat, beat in vanilla and pour into greased tin. Cool slightly
before marking into squares.

 # Horehound Cough Candy

Preparation time: 5 minutes
Cooking time: about 20 minutes

Molly's father used to make this and the following peppermint creams during the winter. They are both extremely easy to make. The oil of horehound is obtainable from chemist shops (drugstores).

Imperial (Metric)	American
1 lb soft brown sugar	*2½ cups soft brown sugar*
2 tablespoons golden syrup	*2 tablespoons maple syrup*
3 drops oil of horehound	*3 drops oil of horehound*
¼ pint (150 ml) water	*just over ½ cup water*

1. Boil the syrup, sugar and water until it forms a soft ball in cold water. stir in the oil of horehound, remove from the heat and beat until the mixture thickens.
2. Pour into a buttered tin and mark into squares when it cools. It separates easily when cold.

This candy, like treacle toffee, was always made when someone had a cough or a sore throat.

 # Dad's Peppermint Creams

Preparation time: 30 minutes
Cooking time: nil

Imperial (Metric)	American
12 oz (350 g) caster sugar	*1½ cups caster sugar*
1 egg white	*1 egg white*
few drops peppermint essence	*few drops peppermint essence*
icing sugar	*confectioner's sugar*

1. Beat egg white until stiff then add the caster sugar and the peppermint. Continue beating until it forms a thick fondant mixture.
2. Sprinkle icing sugar on a marble slab or smooth work surface, turn out the fondant and knead lightly with the fingers. Roll out to ¼ in (5 mm) thick and cut out rounds with a 1 in (2.5 cm) cutter. If the mixture becomes too crumbly, scrape it into a pan and gently heat until it softens. Knead and roll out all scraps to make more creams and place the finished ones on greaseproof paper on a tray. Leave at least overnight in a warm place to dry out completely.

The peppermints make attractive presents either in a round plastic box or in a small bag tied with ribbon.

If you want to make something more special try coating them with melted chocolate — melted in a bowl over hot water. You can either half-coat by holding the peppermint with tongs and diping half into the chocolate or place the peppermints on a metal grid over a baking tin and spoon chocolate over them. The surplus chocolate will drip through the grid. This is rather messy but becomes easier with practice.

An American aunt of Molly's mother brought the following recipe back to England during the Edwardian period and it has been back across the Atlantic many times since.

 # Auntie's Nut and Cherry Bars

Preparation time: 10 minutes
Cooking time: about 20 minutes

Imperial (Metric)

1 lb (450 g) granulated sugar
2 oz (50 g) chopped nuts
2 oz (50 g) glacé cherries
1 teaspoon cream of tartar
1 teaspoon vanilla essence
1/4 pint (150 ml) water
2 teaspoons butter

American

2 cups granulated sugar
1/2 cup chopped nuts
1/2 cup glacé cherries
1 teaspoon cream of tartar
1 teaspoon vanilla essence
just over 1/2 cup water
2 teaspoons butter

1. Cook sugar, water, butter and cream of tartar to soft ball stage. Leave to cool a little then beat in vanilla essence until mixture thickens.
2. Stir in fruit and nuts and turn into a greased tray. Mark into bars before it hardens. When completely cold, break into bars, wrap in foil and store in tin.

 # Coconut Ice

Preparation time: 20 minutes
Cooking time: 10 minutes

This looks splendid piled high on a long stemmed cake plate or coupe dish. If you like, you can divide the mixture into three and add a few drops of pink or green colouring to two of the parts.

Imperial (Metric)

1 lb (450 g) granulated sugar
1/2 pint (275 ml) water
1/2 lb (225 g) dessicated coconut

American

2 cups white sugar
1 1/3 cups water
2 cups dessicated coconut

1. Boil sugar and water in a heavy bottomed pan for 10 minutes. Add coconut and beat until thick and creamy.
2. Pour into greased tins. Leave to get cold before carefully cutting into cubes.

Presentation is half the battle if you are going to give sweets as gifts and we save any small clear plastic boxes and lengths of ribbon or rosettes that may be suitable. One that our friends seem particularly to enjoy receiving is a recipe from Molly's father for Brandy Truffles. These are very rich and we treat them as a luxury item. They keep well in a screw top jar, but rarely get the chance.

 ## Brandy Truffles

Preparation time: 30 minutes
Cooking time: 5 minutes

Imperial (Metric)	American
4 oz (110 g) best dark bitter chocolate	*¼ lb best dark chocolate*
4 oz (110 g) ginger biscuits (see recipe on p. 140)	*4 oz ginger biscuits (see recipe on p. 140)*
2 tablespoons double cream	*2 tablespoons heavy cream*
1 tablespoon brandy	*1 tablespoon brandy*
6 oz (175 g) icing sugar	*just under 1 cup icing sugar*

1. Melt the chocolate in a basin over hot water. Remove from heat and stir in cream and brandy, then add ginger biscuits ground to a powder and gradually stir in sugar. Mix until you have a smooth stiff paste.
2. Coat hands with icing sugar and roll very small teaspoonsful of the mixture into balls. Leave to harden on a large tray.

For a special present we roll some in icing sugar, some in chocolate vermicelli and some in coloured sugar strands. They are a bit fiddly and time consuming to make but are well worth the effort. This quantity makes about four dozen truffles.

Biscuits or Cookies

There was time when few people apart from country folk made their own biscuits because they were so cheap to buy in the shops. In 1939, for instance, you could buy 8 lb of mixed fancy biscuits for a pound note and at half a crown (12½ p) for 1 lb there was no way a housewife could match the bought article for variety.

Today in most countries, the price of even the plainest biscuits has gone through the roof, and the cost of the fancier sort is prohibitive for people on limited incomes. Here again the main factor has been the increase in labour costs and, although fuel and ingredients have to be taken into account, you can still save a great deal of money by making good quality biscuits for your own consumption and to give as presents. Here is a selection of our favourite biscuits − tried and tested recipes from family and friends.

This recipe for Ginger Biscuits came from Molly's Aunt Evelyn and is possibly the most useful one we've ever come across. We use it for the base of cheesecakes, for making brandy truffles and other sweets and adapt it to make several alternative biscuits.

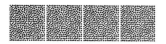 # Aunt Evelyn's Ginger Biscuits

Preparation time: 20 minutes
Cooking time: 10 minutes each batch

Imperial (Metric)	**American**
12 oz (350 g) self-raising flour	*3 cups self-rising flour*
6 oz (175 g) margarine	*¾ cup margarine*
2 tablespoons golden syrup	*2 tablespoons maple syrup*
1 egg	*1 egg*
8 oz (225 g) granulated sugar	*1 cup granulated sugar*
2 teaspoons ginger	*2 teaspoons ginger*
1 teaspoon bicarbonate of soda	*1 teaspoon bicarbonate of soda*

1. Melt margarine, syrup and sugar in a pan. Mix flour, bicarb and ginger in a bowl.
2. Pour melted mixture over flour and stir. Add beaten egg. Stir to a soft dough.
3. When cool take tiny pinches with floured hands and roll into small balls about the size of a nutmeg. Place wide apart on a greased baking tray: 16 biscuits fit on a full sized tray. Flatten biscuits slightly and cook at 350°F/180°C/Gas Mark 4 for ten minutes. For economy with fuel, fill four trays and move them up in the oven as the top one is ready. If you have a fan-assisted oven they should all be ready at the same time.

This quantity makes about 100 biscuits. They keep well but you can also freeze them putting ten at a time in small bags. They don't need reheating, simply defrost for about one hour.

Variations
1. Almond Biscuits — Omit ginger and 6 oz flour and replace by 6 oz ground almonds and 3 drops of almond essence.
2. Oatmeal Biscuits — Omit ginger and 6 oz flour and replace by 6 oz oatmeal.
3. Coconut Biscuits — Omit 6 oz flour and ginger and replace by 6 oz dessicated coconut.

Vary biscuits by placing flaked almond, raisin or sliver of glacé cherry on top before cooking.

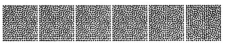 # Crunch Biscuits

Preparation time: 10 minutes to mix. About 20 minutes to roll biscuits
Cooking time: 15 minutes per tray

This quantity makes 72 biscuits — six trays.

Imperial (Metric)	American
4 oz (110 g) dessicated coconut	*1 cup dessicated coconut*
4 oz (110 g) fine oatmeal	*1 cup rolled oats*
4 oz (110 g) wholemeal flour	*1 cup whole wheat flour*
4 oz (110 g) margarine	*½ cup margarine*
4 oz (110 g) soft brown sugar	*½ cup soft brown sugar*
2 tablespoons golden syrup	*2 tablespoons maple syrup*
1 teaspoon mixed spice	*1 teaspoon mixed spice*
1 teaspoon bicarbonate of soda	*1 teaspoon bicarbonate of soda*
1 egg, beaten	*1 egg, beaten*

1. Mix together coconut, oatmeal and flour in a bowl. Heat margarine, sugar, syrup and spice until runny. Remove from heat, cool slightly and beat in egg.
2. Dissolve bicarbonate of soda in 1 tablespoon hot water, add to margarine mixture, stir well then pour into the flour and coconut. Stir well.
3. Flour hands and roll small balls of mixture. Place 12 at a time on a large greased biscuit or oven tray and bake in moderate oven (375°F/190°C/Gas Mark 5) for 15 minutes.

These are very filling.

Another version was given to us by an old friend. These are more like flapjacks and are cut into pieces after cooking.

 # Toffee Crunch Biscuits

Preparation time: 10 minutes
Cooking time: 15 minutes

Imperial (Metric)	American
4 oz (110 g) jumbo oats	*1 cup jumbo oats*
tablespoon fine oats	*tablespoon fine oats*
4 oz (110 g) margarine	*½ cup margarine*
3 oz (75 g) demarara sugar	*3 level tablespoons soft brown sugar*

1. Mix oats and sugar. Melt margarine and mix with oats mixture. Press into a greased shallow tin 11 in x 7 in (28 cm x 18 cm).
2. Bake in preheated oven (375°F/190°C/Gas Mark 5) for 15 minutes. Cut into 12 while still slightly warm but leave in tin until quite cold.

Variation

Dip the biscuits into melted chocolate. You need 4 oz (110 g) bar of milk or plain chocolate melted in a basin over hot water. If you hold each biscuit with a pair of tongs you can dip them safely or you can place them on a tray and carefully pour the chocolate over one side. Leave to set completely on a wire grid.

 Basic Biscuits

Preparation time: 10 minutes

Cooking time: 50 minutes

Another useful biscuit made by the rolling method comes from Molly's mother's recipe book.

Imperial (Metric)	**American**
2 oz (50 g) margarine	*4 level tablespoons margarine*
3 oz (75 g) wholemeal flour	*3 heaped tablespoons wholewheat flour*
1 oz (25 g) dessicated coconut	*1 heaped tablespoon dessicated coconut*
2 tablespoons rolled oats	*2 tablespoons rolled oats*
2 tablespoons chopped nuts	*2 tablespoons chopped nuts*
2 oz (50 g) granulated sugar	*2 level tablespoons granulated sugar*
1 tablespoon milk	*1 tablespoon milk*

1. Rub margarine into flour then mix in all other ingredients. Mix until you have a dough like consistency. Roll out on a floured board.
2. Cut into small rounds and bake on a greased tray in slow oven 300°F/150°C/ Gas Mark 2 for about 50 minutes.

Variations
1. Replace nuts by currants.
2. Replace nuts by pieces of glacé cherries.
3. Sandwich two together with vanilla icing (see below).

 Custard Creams

Preparation time: 20 minutes

Cooking time: 10 minutes

We have no idea how long these biscuits will keep. However many we make, they vanish in a flash.

Imperial (Metric)	**American**
4 oz (110 g) self-raising flour	*1 cup self-rising flour*

8 oz (225 g) custard powder	½ lb custard powder
8 oz (225 g) icing sugar	1½ cups icing sugar
8 oz (225 g) soft butter	1 cup butter
2 egg yolks	2 egg yolks
1 teaspoon vanilla essence	1 teaspoon vanilla essence

1. Sieve icing sugar and flour into a large bowl and mix in butter. Using a fork or a mixer blend in all the other ingredients until you get a smooth dough. Roll out thinly on a floured board and cut into small rounds.

2. Place on a greased baking tray and bake for ten minutes at 375°F/190°C/Gas Mark 5. When cool sandwich together.

Vanilla Icing

Imperial (Metric)

4 oz (110 g) butter
6 oz (175 g) icing sugar
2 teaspoons hot water
1 teaspoon vanilla essence

American

½ cup butter
just over 1 cup icing sugar
2 teaspoons hot water
1 teaspoon vanilla essence

Beat all ingredients with a fork or electric whisk until smooth and fluffy. Use to sandwich biscuits together.

Variations

1. Lemon Creams — Add dessertspoon finely grated lemon rind to biscuit dough. For lemon filling omit vanilla, add 2 teaspoons lemon juice and 2 teaspoons finely grated lemon rind.

2. Chocolate Creams — Add dessertspoon finely grated dark chocolate to biscuit dough. For chocolate filling, add 1 dessertspoon grated dark chocolate.

3. Coffee Creams — Add 1 teaspoon instant coffee powder to biscuit dough. For coffee filling, add 2 teaspoons instant coffee powder.

 # Chocolate Sponge Fingers

Preparation time: 15 minutes
Cooking time: 10 minutes

Imperial (Metric)

2 eggs
2 oz (50 g) caster sugar
2 oz (50 g) self-raising flour
small bar dark chocolate

American

2 eggs
2 tablespoons sugar
½ cup self-rising flour
small bar dark chocolate

1. Grease sponge finger tins, dust with a little flour.

2. Beat or whisk eggs and sugar until thick and creamy. Sift flour and fold in gently.

3. Half fill sponge finger tins and bake at 325°F/170°C/Gas Mark 3 for 10 minutes. Cool slightly in tins then lift out very carefully onto wire grid.

4. Melt chocolate in basin over hot water, dip one end of biscuits in melted chocolate and leave on wire grid until set. Eat within two days.

Digestive Biscuits

Preparation time: 20 minutes
Cooking time: about 20 minutes

Although we always think of digestives as plain biscuits, it's surprising how versatile they are. You can sandwich them with butter cream, dip them in chocolate or eat them with cheese. We always try to have a tin of these on hand.

Imperial (Metric)

8 oz (225 g) wholemeal flour
1 oz (25 g) soft brown sugar
4 oz (110 g) soft margarine
½ teaspoon bicarbonate of soda
1 egg yolk
3 tablespoons milk

American

2 cups wholewheat flour
1 tablespoon soft brown sugar
½ cup soft margarine
½ teaspoon bicarbonate of soda
1 egg yolk
3 tablespoons milk

1. Mix all dry ingredients in a bowl. Rub in the margarine. Mix in the milk and egg yolk until it becomes a soft dough.
2. Knead until smooth then turn out on a floured board and roll out very thinly.
3. Cut out biscuits with a 2 in (5 cm) cutter and place on a greased baking tray. Bake for 20 minutes at 350°F/180°C/Gas Mark 4 until slightly golden.

Shortbread Biscuits

Preparation time: 20 minutes
Cooking time: 20 minutes

Imperial (Metric)

4 oz (110 g) unsalted butter
2 oz (50 g) caster sugar
6 oz (175 g) plain flour

American

½ cup unsalted butter
2 tablespoons caster sugar
1½ cups all purpose flour

1. Warm the mixing bowl, then put in the butter and beat it with a wooden spoon. Slowly add the sugar and then the flour, beating all the time until it binds together.
2. Turn the dough onto a floured board and roll out to ¼ in thick (5 mm). Cut rounds with fluted 2 in (5 cm) cutter, place very carefully on greased baking trays − they are rather fragile − and prick the top of each biscuit with a fork. Bake at 325°F/170°C/Gas Mark 3 for 20 minutes. Cool on a wire grid and sprinkle with caster sugar.

You can also make a large biscuit, cutting it by pressing down a bowl on the rolled pastry. Mark it lightly into triangles before cooking and separate carefully when cold. The large one will take approximately ten minutes extra baking or until it starts to colour slightly.

A friend in her eighties gave us this recipe for plain tea biscuits which is very economical. They are also excellent with cheese.

Plain Tea Biscuits

Preparation time: 15 minutes
Cooking time: 20 minutes

Imperial (Metric)

1 lb (450 g) plain flour
1 egg yolk
enough milk to make a very stiff dough

American

4 cups all purpose flour
1 egg yolk
enough milk to make a very stiff dough

Mix egg and flour. Add a little milk very slowly and knead until smooth. Roll out on a floured board until very thin and cut into small biscuits. Bake at 300°F/150°C/Gas Mark 2 until crisp.

An Irish friend gave us this recipe for water biscuits which has now become one of our most useful standbys.

Traditional Irish Water Biscuits

Preparation time: 15 minutes
Cooking time: 10 minutes per batch

Imperial (Metric)

2 lbs (900 g) plain flour
2 oz (50 g) butter
½ pint (275 ml) milk
pinch salt

American

8 cups all purpose flour
4 tablespoons butter
1⅓ cups milk
pinch salt

Mix the sifted flour and salt together. Heat the butter and milk until the butter melts. Pour into the flour and mix to a smooth dough. Roll out very thinly on a floured board. Use a small square cutter for biscuits and place them on lightly greased baking trays. Prick the biscuits with a small fork and bake for about ten minutes at 400°F/200°C/Gas Mark 6.

We have found the following curry biscuits go surprisingly well with smoked mackerel or smoked salmon pâté, although they are very tasty just with butter.

 ## Curry Biscuits

Preparation time: 15 minutes
Cooking time: 10 minutes

Imperial (Metric)

2 oz (50 g) ground rice
2 oz (50 g) plain flour
1 oz (25 g) margarine
1 teaspoon curry powder
1 teaspoon sesame seeds
water to mix

American

2 heaped tablespoons ground rice
2 heaped tablespoons all purpose flour
2 tablespoons margarine
1 teaspoon curry powder
1 teaspoon sesame seeds
water to mix

1. Melt margarine gently and add to dry ingredients. Mix in a little water slowly until you have a stiff dough. Knead until smooth.
2. Roll out very thinly on floured board and cut into small rounds. Place on lightly greased tray and prick all biscuits with a small fork.
3. Bake for ten minutes at 400°F/200°C/Gas Mark 6.

 ## Cheese Straws

Preparation time: about 1 hour
Cooking time: 10 minutes each batch

Don't start to make these unless you have plenty of time, but they are well worth making for a dinner party. They look very impressive arranged in bundles pushed through their cheese rings, they keep very well and they taste so good that you have to put them out at the very last minute or they will vanish.

Imperial (Metric)

8 oz (225 g) plain flour
4 oz (110 g) butter
1 egg, beaten
4 oz (110 g) hard cheese, grated
salt and pepper

American

2 cups all purpose flour
1/2 cup butter
1 egg, beaten
1 cup hard cheese, grated
salt and pepper

1. Rub butter into flour and seasonings until crumbly. Add cheese and mix in well. Stir in the beaten egg and mix to a smooth dough.
2. Turn out on a floured board and knead again. Roll out into a large rectangle ¼ in (5 mm) thick and with a plastic ruler and a sharp knife cut out straws 8 in (20 cm) long. Roll up trimmings into a ball and roll out thinly. Cut into rounds with a 1½ in (4 cm) cutter and then remove the centres with a 1 in (2.5 cm) cutter to make pastry circles.
3. Carefully place circles and cheese straws on lightly greased baking trays and cook for about ten minutes at 400°F/200°C/Gas Mark 6. Check them after eight minutes — they should be pale golden but not browned. Remove onto a wire grid to cool but do this very carefully as they are fragile at this stage.

4. Serve in bundles of straws fitted through circles.

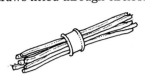

These are delicious on their own, served with soft butter or used with any creamy dip.

Incidentally, if you are going out for the day or on a picnic it's a good idea to pack a few sweets and biscuits quite separately from the main goodies mentioned in the next chapter, especially if you are travelling some distance in the car. You then have something ready to hand for the journey.

11

Eating Out
~ or How to Make
Retirement a Picnic

One thing about retirement that takes some getting used to is the fact that if the sun is shining you can get out for a walk or a drive in the country without worrying about what time you are going to get back.

It needn't cost very much either. Shank's mare costs nothing but shoe leather and, even if you are not yet eligible for Senior Citizen's travel privileges, you can usually travel more cheaply on trains and buses when you no longer have to make your journeys at peak travel times — and you can also take advantage of any cheap excursions or special publicity drive cheap fares.

There's a lot to see and do, but what puts many people off even the simplest excursion is the high cost of eating out. Naturally, if you have been used to expense account lunches, the thought of spending that sort of money out of your own pocket is appalling. However, do not despair. Bread and cheese will keep you going as well as, and perhaps better than, Lobster Thermidor, and if you still want to eat well but do it cheaply you can always take a picnic.

I used to think picnics were only for children until I went to Ireland and met some of the horsey set whose idea of a simple al fresco lunch was a banquet in the boot of the Rolls. However, it wasn't until we went to live in France and watched our Gallic friends enjoying le pique-nique that we realised that outdoor meals had come a long way since our mothers regaled us with hardboiled eggs, ginger beer and fruit cake.

We laughed at first when we saw French families carefully setting up tables and chairs with napkins, sparkling cutlery and wine glasses before unloading a five or six course meal with appropriate wines. Real picnickers, we told ourselves smugly, were happy to sit on a sandy towel eating tinned salmon sandwiches from the obligatory greaseproof paper. It wasn't long, though, before we were converted — at least to the idea that it was possible to enjoy a civilised meal out of doors.

Of course, it doesn't have to be a banquet. If you are just going out for a walk, you may not wish to carry more than a couple of sandwiches, but this doesn't mean that your packed lunches have to be dreary. Now that you have time for a little extra preparation you can make the most light weight meals tasty and attractive.

Pocket Size Meals

An apple and a bar of chocolate or a few home-made sweets in a bag are a good source of energy for an improvised picnic during a short walk, but when you start to think in terms of something to drink it becomes a bit more difficult to fit in the pocket. A good thirst quenching idea used by an old friend is to peel an orange, divide into segments and put three or four in a small plastic bag. Seal the top and pop into the pocket for an instant light weight 'drink'. The other pieces will keep in the refrigerator in another bag. Or you could take one of those little drink cartons, that come complete with their own straw. They are available in a wide variety of flavours.

Of course, if you are going to take a small shoulder bag you could fit in the tiny size of vacuum flask with a hot or cold drink depending on the weather but, assuming you just want to use your pockets, here are a few suggestions.

Sandwiches

Moist fillings are best for these as nothing is more off putting than dry curling bread with a dry piece of cheese or meat. Try:

Cream cheese with chopped parsley or chives. Spread right to the edges of brown bread.

Tinned salmon, tuna or sardines, mashed with butter and lemon juice.
Soft boiled eggs chopped with skinned tomatoes and mashed with butter.
Pâtés — such as smoked mackerel, mushroom or liver pâté with a little extra low fat margarine.

Always put on a bit more filling than you would for a sandwich at home and cut into quarters. Divide the sandwiches into two small bags — one for each pocket — so that one lot will keep moist while you are eating the first.

Fruit fillings. These are surprisingly refreshing. Try:

Grated apple, a squeeze of lemon juice, on brown bread with low fat spread or butter.
Chopped raisins mixed with cream cheese on brown bread.
Chopped pineapple (if canned, drain well) mixed with cream cheese on brown bread.

Desserts
Apples of course are perfect but try the orange segments as suggested above or a small bag of raisins. The very small polythene cartons with snap on lid will fit into a pocket and will hold a few fresh fruits such as strawberries, raspberries or cherries and, if you also slip a small plastic spoon in your pocket, you could try puréed fruit or some chopped canned peaches or apricots. These are all refreshing if you can't get a drink.

If you are walking, the secret is to carry as little as you can which means that whenever possible liquids — which are very heavy — should be obtained as close as possible to where you are going to eat. This may require a little reconnaissance if the place is going to be a regular picnic spot. There may be a farm where you can obtain milk, or a café which provides take-away cartons of tea or coffee or a van which sells ice cream or drinks.

If you are going on a long walk it's worth making a detour through a village or past a farm which sells produce. After all it's a bit ridiculous to carry expensive fruit for miles and then come to signs inviting you to pick your own for a few pence.

Light Packed Lunches

If you don't mind carrying a shoulder bag or you are travelling by bike — or even by bus or train — you can take a bit more than a pocketful. But you still won't wish to be encumbered by a full scale picnic.

Try adding one interesting main course at least to your snack, and take along a flask with a cold or hot drink. Home-made lemonade in hot weather is particularly refreshing and either soup or hot chocolate seems perfect whenever there's a nip in the air.

A large napkin will serve as a table cloth for your mini feast and will make you feel quite civilised.

A substantial slice of quiche makes a good choice for a main course or you could try a Cornish Pasty. Small pies — meat, cheese or fruit — are ideal because they can be eaten with the fingers. Auntie Nell's recipe (see p. 74) is a useful one for these.

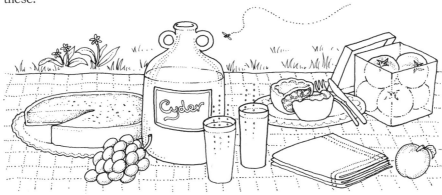

Home-made Lemonade

Preparation time: 5 minutes
Cooking time: 2 minutes

This makes 2½ pints (1.4 litres) of concentrate which keeps well in tightly sealed bottles. Dilute to taste.

Imperial (Metric)

juice and grated rind of 2 large lemons
1½ lb (700 g) granulated sugar
1 oz (25 g) citric acid
1½ pints (850 ml) boiling water

American

juice and grated rind of 2 large lemons
3 cups granulated sugar
1 oz or tablespoon citric acid
3¾ cups boiling water

Put juice and grated rind of lemon in pan of boiling water. Add other ingredients and stir for two minutes until sugar has dissolved. Remove from heat, allow to cool and bottle.

For a picnic, dilute to taste, chill and add a mint leaf before putting in flask.

 # Cornish Pasty (To make two)

Preparation time: 40 minutes, including making pastry
Cooking time: about 45 minutes
Shortcrust pastry

Imperial (Metric)	American
4 oz (110 g) plain flour	*1 cup all purpose flour*
2 oz (50 g) vegetable fat or mixture of butter and fat	*¼ cup vegetable fat or mixture of butter and fat*
2 tablespoons water	*2 tablespoons water*
pinch of salt	*pinch of salt*

1. Blend butter into sifted flour first with knife and then with fingers until it becomes crumbly.
2. Make a well in centre and add water. Blend using fork until the dough comes together in a ball, leaving the bowl clean. Turn out on to a floured work surface and knead for one minute.

Filling

4 oz (110 g) very lean beef steak	*¼ lb tender lean beef steak*
1 large potato	*1 large potato*
1 small onion	*1 small onion*
1 small turnip	*1 small turnip*
¼ teaspoon mixed dried herbs	*¼ teaspoon mixed dried herbs*
salt and pepper	*salt and pepper*
1 teaspoon water or stock	*1 tablespoon water or stock*

1. Remove any fat from meat and shred into small matchsticks. Peel and chop onion, and peel and cut into small dice both turnip and potato. Mix all together with herbs, seasoning and stock.
2. Divide dough into two. Roll out each portion to a circle about 6 in (15 cm). Divide filling into two and place in centre of pastry circles. Damp edges and draw up two opposite sides to meet over filling. Crimp edges, brush with a little milk and place on baking tray. Bake at 400°F/200°C/Gas Mark 6 for 15 minutes, then reduce heat to 375°F/190°C/Gas Mark 5 for about 30 minutes.

If you want to cook them more quickly you can prepare filling then bring it to the boil in a little more stock, reduce heat and simmer for 20 minutes. This can be cooking while you make the pastry. Add the cooked filling and proceed as before, except that you need only bake the pasties for 15 minutes or until golden brown at the first heat.

Variations
1. Fill with a mixture of chopped boiled onion (1 large), 4 oz (110 g) (1 cup) grated cheese and black pepper. Proceed as above and bake for 15 minutes.
2. Vegetable: fill with mixture of 1 medium potato, 1 medium carrot, 1 medium onion, chopped and boiled. Add black pepper, salt, ½ teaspoon mixed dried herbs and few chopped mushrooms. Proceed as above and bake for 15 minutes or until golden.
3. Vegetable curry. To vegetable ingredients add 1 teaspoon curry powder moistened with a little stock plus a few cooked peas.

All of these are quite substantial. We find they travel well if wrapped in foil or packed in a lightweight plastic box. Cornish miners used to eat large pasties which had meat and potato at one end and jam or fruit filling at the other, separated by a dividing wall of pastry. If you are a regular picnicker it might be worth experimenting with this!

Of course for a plate pie you simply double the quantity of shortcrust pastry.

Cheese and Onion Plate Pie

Preparation time: 30 minutes
Cooking time: 25−30 minutes

Imperial (Metric)

8 oz (225 g) shortcrust pastry
1 large onion
8 oz (225 g) cheddar cheese, grated
salt and pepper

American

8 oz shortcrust pastry
1 large onion
2 cups cheddar cheese, grated
salt and pepper

1. Divide pastry into two. Grease shallow pie plate (9 inch/23 cm). Roll out one piece of pastry, line plate, cover with greaseproof paper, weight with dried beans and cook blind in hot oven for 10 minutes.
2. Chop onion, boil for ten minutes in a little water until soft. Drain well.
3. Remove pie plate from oven, pile onion on pastry, season, then add grated cheese. Damp pastry rim and cover with second piece of pastry. Trim and press edges to seal.
4. Bake for 25 to 30 minutes until pastry is golden brown at 400°F/200°C/Gas Mark 6.

 # Scotch Eggs

Preparation time: 20 minutes
Cooking time: about 25 minutes

These are great picnic food — satisfying and easy to carry. Two each is plenty.

Imperial (Metric)

4 eggs
½ lb (225 g) sausage meat
a little flour
½ teaspoon dried sage
1 egg, beaten
salt and pepper
enough toasted breadcrumbs to coat
vegetable oil for frying

American

4 eggs
½ lb ground sausage meat
a little flour
½ teaspoon dried sage
1 beaten egg
salt and pepper
enough toasted breadcrumbs to coat
vegetable oil for frying

1. Hardboil the four eggs, cool and shell.
2. Roll the eggs in seasoned flour.
3. Mix sage with sausage meat then divide meat into four pieces. Press out on a floured board to about 3 in x 5 in (7.5 x 13 cm) each piece. Put an egg in the centre of each and carefully press sausage meat all around until egg is completely covered. Meat should be smoothly moulded.
4. Dip into beaten egg and then roll in breadcrumbs. Deep fry for five minutes then drain on absorbent paper and leave to get cold. Eat same day.

Variations

Instead of sausagemeat, use a mixture of grated cheese and mashed potato which will mould nicely around the eggs. Then dip in beaten egg and breadcrumbs and proceed as above.

We find slices of tomato and cucumber in a little French dressing with black pepper and chopped fresh mint travel well in a tiny plastic container, and go very nicely with either of the above.

Picnic Parties

If you have a car you can go in for the real thing — a genuine old-fashioned picnic which can range from an open air children's party on the beach or in the country, to the sort of splendid meal one might expect to be given on a first class shoot. If you don't have a car, you may find that cooking in retirement could help provide transport because, once you get a reputation for making super picnics, you could find plenty of people willing to offer you a day out in the country in return for preparing some of the food.

For this sort of picnic some equipment is preferable. Most picnics are for numbers ranging from two to ten and, as you won't want to travel to the country or the seaside with your best bone china and delicate champagne flutes, it's as well to have a few special items.

We find that for most family picnics the following equipment is well worth having:

A cool box or bag. These utilise ice bags which are stored in the freezer and will keep your whole meal, including wine or soft drinks, beautifully cool. It is almost worth buying one just to have a crisp lettuce on a picnic. Despite their name, they will also keep food hot if you boil the little bags instead of freezing them but unless you are having a skating party it's usually better to have a barbecue if you want hot food.

Large heavy quality plastic cloth. We have a red and white checked monster which is cheerful to look at and heavy enough not to flap about in the wind. It also sponges off easily — which means you don't have to worry about children, or grown ups for that matter, spilling things. We use it on a big old garden table, too, for eating out in summer.

Plastic plates, cups, 'glasses', etc. You can now buy quite substantial knives, forks and so on that weigh next to nothing and cost very little, and while I have to confess that I prefer my wine in a proper glass I will make the sacrifice if I have to and it's better than breaking glasses and cutting fingers on a picnic.

Plastic boxes with close fitting lids in various sizes. These give your picnic a new dimension by enabling you to take along things like mixed salads and squishy desserts.

A couple of vacuum flasks. These can be used for keeping things hot or cold but, when you come right down to it, there's not a lot to beat a good cup of tea in the great outdoors and you can make a fresh one with a tiny gas camping stove.

A shopping trolley. If you are likely to be walking any distance from the car to your picnic site along reasonably flat surfaces a trolley will hold not only the food and drink but a rug and a couple of cushions or folding stools as well.

It's also a good idea for people without a car who want a day out in the park or want to picnic while fishing on a nearby river bank. A small trolley will take a surprising amount of stuff and is quite easy to handle provided the paths are not too steep.

Children's Picnic Food

Picnic food for children shouldn't be too messy or potentially too upsetting, especially if the children in question are going to travel in your car! Favourites, we find, are things like vast quantities of home-made crisps which are easily made by shaving bits off a large potato with a peeler, dropping them into hot fat inside a wire basket and draining on absorbent paper. Sprinkle with a little salt and give each child a large bagful.

 Savoury Swiss Rolls

The variations on this theme are endless but somehow most children seem to prefer them to ordinary sandwiches. Simply spread filling on a slice of bread with the crusts removed and roll up the bread tightly. Wrap each in stretch plastic. If possible, let each child choose fillings for three or four so they can't claim 'There's nothing here I can eat.' Do the same thing with small French loaves, letting each child choose the filling. If you have no idea what they like, you'll have to stick to general favourites like tinned salmon, tuna or cream cheese but it's much better if you know that one child will be happy all afternoon on a diet of mashed banana and peanut butter.

We find that patty tin size meat pies and cheese and onion ones are great faovurites, as well as sausage rolls.

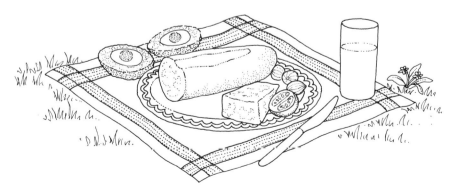

 # Small Sausage Rolls

Make up a batch of flaky pastry for these. Incidentally, this is also the best pastry for traditional Steak and Kidney Pie. Don't forget that when a recipe calls for 1 lb or ½ lb of pastry it refers to the amount of flour used and not to the weight of the finished pastry. Until I was told this basic fact of cookery, I used to wonder why recipes never quite worked out as I'd hoped.

Flaky Pastry
To make ½ lb (225 g)

Total time including resting − about 1½ hours

Imperial (Metric)	American
8 oz (225 g) plain flour	*2 cups all purpose flour*
6 oz (175 g) butter	*¾ cup butter*
½ teaspoon salt	*½ teaspoon salt*
¼ pint (150 ml) water	*just over ½ cup water*

1. Divide butter into four portions. Rub one portion into sieved flour and salt in a large bowl. Add water and mix to a dough. Turn on to a floured board and knead until smooth. Put in a polythene bag and leave for ten minutes.
2. Roll out to a long rectangle. Mark it into thirds. Take a portion of butter, cut it into small pieces and distribute over ⅔ of pastry. Fold both ends over the centre. Turn pastry clockwise and roll out again to long rectangle. Repeat process, resting dough for 15 minutes each time, until you have used up all the butter. Fold again and leave in a cool place for about 30 minutes.

To make rolls
1. We use small pork sausages and prefer to grill them first until cooked but not very brown. Allow them to cool, then roll out the pastry thinly. Cut into long strips 2½ times as wide as the sausages. Place a line of sausages down the strip, damp one long edge and fold over.
2. With a sharp knife cut between the sausages, separating the rolls.
3. Rinse a baking sheet in cold water, place rolls on it and make a small slash on each one with a sharp knife. Brush with milk.
4. Bake at 425°F/220°C/Gas Mark 7 for ten minutes until golden brown and risen.

 # Kebabs

Long skewers with cheese, fruit, cucumber etc. seem to go down well with both children and adults and you can vary them according to what fruits are in season. If you use apples or pears it's best to soak the pieces in a little lemon juice before threading them on the skewers: this stops them from browning.

Try to cut the fruit and cheese into neat squares − pineapple always looks good − and try a few grapes, black or green, or olives to alternate with the squares.

Adult Picnics

For a simple picnic try a few home-made rolls or a crusty loaf, a pot of garlic butter, a hunk of cheese, perhaps a couple of slices of a savoury egg and sausage pie and a dish of whatever fruit is in season. Add a good cake and a bottle of cider and you have the makings of an enjoyable meal.

 # Garlic Butter

Imperial (Metric)

clove of garlic or 2 teaspoons garlic
   paste
4 oz (110 g) butter
1 tablespoon chopped parsley

American

clove of garlic or 2 teaspoons garlic
   paste
1/2 cup butter
1 tablespoon chopped parsley

1. Mash everything together thoroughly,. Put in small covered pot and chill.
2. Keep in cool bag until required on picnic and use on crusty bread.

Variations

1. Cheese spread — grate 2 oz (50 g) (1/2 cup) cheese and add to garlic butter.
2. Aubergine spread — slice an aubergine (eggplant) lengthwise and grill (broil) until soft. Remove flesh and mash with garlic butter and a squeeze of lemon juice.

 # Savoury Egg and Sausage Loaf

Preparation time: 20 minutes

Cooking time: 1 1/2 hours

This is a favourite for picnics as it cuts well and doesn't fall to bits in your hand. It's also a good hot supper dish at home with tomato and basil sauce.

Imperial (Metric)

1 lb (450 g) pork sausagemeat
2 medium onions
4 oz (110 g) mushrooms
3 hardboiled eggs
3 thick slices from white loaf
2 tablespoons fresh parsley, chopped
1/2 teaspoon oregano
1/2 teaspoon dried basil
1 dessertspoon tomato purée
3 tablespoons milk
salt and black pepper
1 egg, beaten

American

1 lb pork sausagemeat
2 medium onions
1/4 lb mushrooms
3 hardboiled eggs
3 thick slices from white loaf
2 tablespoons fresh parsley, chopped
1/2 teaspoon oregano
1/2 teaspoon dried basil
1 dessertspoon tomato purée
3 tablespoons milk
salt and black pepper
1 egg, beaten

1. Chop onions and mushroom finely and put in a large bowl with tomato purée and mashed up sausagemeat. Cut crusts off bread and break into small pieces.

Mash with milk then drain off excess milk and add bread to meat mixture. Stir in seasoning and herbs and then the beaten egg, thoroughly mixing all together.

2. Take a large loaf tin (2 lb (900 g) size) and spread a layer of the mixture in the bottom. Then place the shelled hardboiled eggs in a line down the middle of the layer. Cover with more mixture pressing it around the eggs and finally smooth off the top.

3. Bake in the oven at 375°F/190°C/Gas Mark 5 for 1½ hours.

4. Leave in tin until absolutely cold then turn out onto a sheet of foil and wrap it tightly until required for picnic.

Variations

1. Mushroom and courgette (zucchini) — Replace meat by ½ lb (225 g) courgettes (zucchini) lightly sautéed then mixed with other ingredients. Increase chopped mushrooms to ¾ lb (350 g). Proceed as before.

2. Cheese and mushroom — Replace meat by ¾ lb (350 g) (3 cups) grated cheese and increase chopped mushrooms to ½ lb (225 g). Proceed as before.

All the loaves will slice well and are particularly good between two slices of crusty bread.

A small green salad in a plastic bag in the cooler box and a separate bottle of ready mixed French dressing will turn any of them into a feast.

The flans, tea breads and biscuits from other chapters are also excellent for picnics; but unless it's a special occasion, don't try to do anything elaborate for a picnic. Good fresh ingredients and a little bit of thought are the main things.

Gourmet Picnics

Once in a while — for somebody's birthday perhaps or when distant friends visit and you want to show them a local beauty spot — you may want to make a special effort for a picnic.

For the first course have a choice of perhaps three items: (1) Smoked Salmon or Smoked Mackerel Pâté, (2) Avocado Pâté and (3) Crunchy Sesame Chick Peas. Have white and brown crusty bread, plenty of butter, including a pot of garlic butter, and perhaps a tin of sesame crackers.

For the main course you could try: (1) Layered Fish Terrine, (2) Chicken joints basted with orange juice, (3) Rice Salad or Rainbow Bean Salad and (4) Leek and Cheese Puffs. Add some jars of olives, some large tomatoes from the garden and a large green salad.

If it's the middle of the strawberry season there's no problem about dessert, because an immense bowl of fresh strawberries sprinkled with caster sugar always meets with approval. Otherwise, try any fresh fruit purée from the freezer mixed with curd cheese and a little sugar to make a firm mousse. This will travel well in a sealed container. A fresh fruit salad is another good picnic dessert, especially if you have added a good glass of sherry or brandy to the concoction.

One of our more successful picnics finished with a huge batch of home-made scones. Molly brought two jars of home-made strawberry jam and a carton of clotted cream — this last item having to be purchased — we haven't yet got around to keeping a cow.

We piled on the jam and cream and everyone thoroughly enjoyed it; but the secret with something simple like this is that you must have enough for healthy outdoor appetites. A good selection of home-made cakes is always appreciated too — things like ginger breads and fruit cakes which are not too messy and are pleasantly filling. We like to make up an orange butter with a hint of ginger to keep in a small container. It spices up plain ginger bread into cake for a special occasion, and can be spread on the slices as they are cut.

Scones

Preparation time: 10 minutes
Cooking time: 10 minutes

Imperial (Metric)

8 oz (225 g) self-raising flour
½ teaspoon salt
2 oz (50 g) butter
milk to mix

American

2 cups self-rising flour
½ teaspoon salt
¼ cup butter
milk to mix

1. Sift flour and salt, rub in butter and mix to a soft dough with a little milk.
2. Knead on a floured board then roll out to ½ inch (1 cm) thickness. Cut into rounds with small cutter and bake at 450°F/230°C/Gas Mark 8 for 10 minutes.

 # Bakewell Tart

Preparation time: 30 minutes
Cooking time: 30 minutes

This is a teatime favourite but also carries well for picnics.

Imperial (Metric)

4 oz (110 g) shortcrust pastry
2 oz (50 g) butter
1 oz (25 g) plain flour
2 oz (50 g) ground almonds
2 oz (50 g) caster sugar
1 egg, beaten
level teaspoon baking powder
almond essence
raspberry jam
1 tablespoon milk

American

4 oz shortcrust pastry
¼ cup butter
1 tablespoon all purpose flour
½ cup ground almonds
2 tablespoons caster sugar
1 egg, beaten
level teaspoon baking powder
almond essence
raspberry jam
1 tablespoon milk

1. Roll out pastry and line 7 inch (18 cm) tart tin. Prick base and spread with a little raspberry jam.
2. Cream butter and sugar then add beaten egg and almond essence. Mix flour, baking powder and ground almonds and blend into butter mixture, adding a little milk if necessary.
3. Spread in pastry case and bake for 30 minutes until firm at 350°F/180°C/Gas Mark 4.

 # Treacle Tart

Preparation time: 30 minutes
Cooking time: 25 minutes

Imperial (Metric)

6 oz (175 g) shortcrust pastry
6 rounded tablespoons golden syrup
6 heaped tablespoons fresh white
  breadcrumbs
grated rind and juice of 1 lemon

American

6 oz shortcrust pastry
6 rounded tablespoons maple syrup
6 heaped tablespoons fresh white
  breadcrumbs
grated rind and juice of 1 lemon

1. Roll out pastry on a floured board to line a 10 inch (25 cm) tart tin.
2. Warm the syrup until runny then stir in the breadcrumbs, finely grated lemon rind and lemon juice. Add a few more breadcrumbs if the mixture is too runny. Leave for 5 minutes.
3. Spread carefully in pastry case, and decorate with thin pastry strips arranged in lattice pattern on top.
4. Bake at 400°F/200°C/Gas Mark 6 for 10 minutes then lower to 375°F/190°C/Gas Mark 5 for a further 15 minutes.

Cheesecake is a general favourite. We like this plain variety but you can also top it with fresh fruit and cream if you want a very rich filling.

 # Cheesecake

Preparation time: 10 minutes
Cooking time: 30 minutes

Biscuit base

Imperial (Metric)

8 oz (225 g) ginger biscuits
4 oz (110 g) butter

American

8 oz ginger biscuits
½ cup butter

Filling

1½ lb (700 g) curd cheese
8 oz (225 g) caster sugar
3 eggs
1 teaspoon vanilla essence

1½ lb curd cheese
1 cup caster sugar
3 eggs
1 teaspoon vanilla essence

1. Crush biscuits into fine crumbs. Stir into melted butter. Allow to cool slightly then press evenly on base of a large 10 inch (25 cm) loose-based flan tin.
2. Beat curd cheese, sugar, eggs and vanilla essence to a thick cream and pour over biscuit base, smoothing it carefully.
3. Cook for 30 minutes at 300°F/150°C/Gas Mark 2. Leave to cool then chill overnight.

 # Eccles Cakes

Preparation time: 20 minutes
Cooking time: 20 minutes

These traditional pastries can be made with left over pieces of puff pastry, provided you pile the trimmings one on top of another before rerolling. This maintains the layers of fat and enables the pastry to rise.

Imperial (Metric)	**American**
8 oz (225 g) puff pastry	*8 oz puff pastry*
1 oz (25 g) butter	*2 tablespoons butter*
1 oz (25 g) soft brown sugar	*1 tablespoon soft brown sugar*
1 oz (25 g) chopped peel	*1 tablespoon chopped peel*
4 oz (110 g) currants	*1 cup currants*
finely grated rind of 1 lemon	*finely grated rind of 1 lemon*
1 level teaspoon mixed spice	*1 level teaspoon mixed spice*
milk	*milk*

1. Roll out pastry very thinly. Melt butter over a low heat and stir in all other ingredients. Leave to cool.
2. Cut pastry into rounds using a 4 inch (10 cm) cutter. Depending on thinness of pastry you will get 16 to 18 rounds. Place a teaspoonful of filling in the centre of each, damp the edges, draw them up and squeeze together. Turn the cakes over and gently roll them flat until they measure about 3 inch (7.5 cm). Make three slits across the top of each with a very sharp knife. Brush with milk, sprinkle with a little sugar and place on a baking tray rinsed in cold water. Bake at 425°F/220°C/ Gas Mark 7 for 20 minutes or until golden brown. Cool before eating.

 # Sesame Chick Peas

Preparation time: Soaking overnight
Cooking time: 10 minutes

Imperial (Metric)	**American**
4 oz (110 g) dried chick peas	*¼ lb dried chick peas*
1 tablespoon sesame seeds	*1 tablespoon sesame seeds*
1 tablespoon garam masala	*1 tablespoon garam masala*
1 tablespoon oil	*1 tablespoon oil*
salt	*salt*

1. Soak the chick peas overnight.
2. Rinse and dry the soaked chick peas.
3. Heat the oil in a frying pan until very hot then drop in the sesame seeds and stir. Add the chick peas and turn and shake them around the pan until they are crisp and golden and covered with sesame seeds.
4. Drain on absorbent paper, sprinkle with a mixture of garam masala and salt and, when cool, store in an airtight jar or tin.

Sesame Crackers

Preparation time: 20 minutes
Cooking time: 12 minutes

These crackers, together with the curry biscuits or oatcakes, are excellent with any pâtés.

Imperial (Metric)

4 oz (110 g) sesame seeds
3 oz (75 g) margarine
6 oz (175 g) plain flour
2 teaspoons baking powder
2 eggs
pinch salt

American

¼ lb sesame seeds
6 tablespoons margarine
1½ cups all purpose flour
2 teaspoons baking powder
2 eggs
pinch salt

1. Heat oven to 350°F/180°C/Gas Mark 4 and put sesame seeds on baking tray on top shelf for five minutes. Remove and shake once to turn seeds. Remove them from oven and switch to 375°F/190°C/Gas Mark 5.
2. Rub margarine into flour, baking powder and salt. Add toasted sesame seeds and beat in the eggs. Beat until mixture is smooth.
3. Put small spoonfuls on a greased baking tray and flatten them in the middle. Bake for 12 minutes until golden brown. Cool on a wire grid.

Leek and Cheese Puffs

Preparation time: 25 minutes
Cooking time: 20 minutes

These mouthwatering triangles are perfect for picnics, although they are also a very good starter for a dinner.

Imperial (Metric)

1 lb (450 g) puff pastry or large packet
    frozen
4 medium leeks
4 oz (110 g) grated cheese
2 eggs
salt and black pepper

American

1 lb puff pastry or large packet frozen
4 medium leeks
1 cup grated cheese
2 eggs
salt and black pepper

1. Thaw the pastry if frozen. Wash leeks very thoroughly and cut into 2 in (5 cm) pieces. Poach in salt water for a few minutes. Drain very well and pat dry.
2. Roll out pastry thinly and cut into 12 squares. Place a piece of leek on each square. Put grated cheese in a small bowl and add 1 beaten egg and seasoning. Mix well. Place a spoonful of cheese mixture on each leek and fold over the pastry to make a triangle. Moisten the edges and press down with a fork to crimp them.
3. Beat up the other egg and brush over the tops of the triangles. Bake for 20 minutes at 400°F/200°C/Gas Mark 6 until golden brown.

Variations

1. Mix together ¼ lb (110 g) chopped mushrooms, 1 finely grated small onion and 1 beaten egg. Use as filling.

2. Beat up the flesh of two ripe avocados with 4 oz (110 g) (¼ lb) Danish blue, Stilton or Roquefort cheese. Add black pepper and use to fill pastry.

Picnic drinks are no problem and home-made lemonade is an excellent appetiser and thirst quencher. Canned beer is okay but a bit fizzy; and, besides, I usually find that fetching a bottle or two of ale from the nearest pub takes just about as long as it takes Molly to unpack the food — which seems a fair division of labour.

Generally we find it best to stick to one drink throughout the meal and to give people as little choice as possible, other than between alcoholic and non-alcoholic.

A dryish cider will last the whole meal through as you can drink it with anything and the same goes for champagne or any of the drier sparkling wines. Our favourite though is a nicely chilled rosé which we hardly ever drink indoors but which somehow seems to be the ideal accompaniment to an al fresco meal.

We love picnics, perhaps because there's something about eating in the open air that recalls the endless hot summers of our childhood, but now there's no one to tell us what we should eat — remember how there was never enough of the really nice things? — or not to make a mess.

In fact, we are totally free to decide when and where to go, what to do and what to eat and drink — a freedom which makes picnics in retirement something extra special.

12

Entertaining in Retirement

The marvellous thing about entertaining, once you stop work and take up more amusing things like cooking, is that you rarely have to provide meals for other people unless you want to. There are no bosses in search of ego massage and no subordinates in need of reassurance and a free meal — only family and friends whose visits should be a joy.

They should be a joy — and often will be — but this is yet another advantage of being retired; if you don't feel up to entertaining you can, and should, point any visitors gently in the direction of the most convenient take-away or give them the run of your kitchen!

One thing about entertaining which many retired people have to take into consideration is the cost, but even feeding half a dozen hungry youngsters and their parents needn't be all that expensive. We have one or two recipes which we bring out to feed the five thousand, one of the most useful of which involves using a batter to make beignets with almost everything in the fridge and vegetable rack.

It sounds incredible but you can feed a tremendous number of people on one potato, one large onion, a stick or two of celery, a few mushrooms and so on. And though this sort of meal costs practically nothing, everyone will be convinced they have had a banquet because of the vast amounts of food and the wonderful taste.

Ring the changes by making a sauce of tomato ketchup blended with a little thin cream or the top of the milk, black pepper and a spoonful of sherry or use a tin of condensed mushroom soup with the same additions.

Get the family to help with mixing the batter — use the simple recipe for flour and water batter given on p. 15 — and they can also help with slicing the vegetables paper thin and with deep frying the large batches. You'll need to keep the oven on low to keep everything warm until it's all ready and remember that this is food only for people with iron digestions.

Young people with really big appetites could finish off with apple rings dipped in the same batter and sprinkled with caster sugar. Or you can add the apple rings, without sugar, to the first course.

Another way of coping, particularly with children, is to make stacks of chips (french fries) or home-made crisps (potato chips) both of which are as filling as they are confusing.

Baked in their jacket potatoes are always a success and you can vary them by adding a bit of grated cheese or even baked beans. They are filling and provide a main course without a lot of expense.

You'll also find that your home-made ice creams and fruit sorbets go down well with most young people — and adults, come to think of it — and that they usually enjoy traditional things like Toffee Crunch Biscuits or Grandma's Chocolate Sponge. There's no need to feel that you must empty the supermarket for expensive cakes and desserts.

Incidentally, we once visited an elderly Countess who served us a supper consisting of a huge loaf, a dish of butter and a tin of golden syrup, washed down with large tots of gin — which indicates that there is no social stigma attached to what used to be the food of the poor, provided that you serve it with a bit of panache.

As well as using some of the biscuit recipes we mentioned in a previous chapter, you might like to try some of our favourite cakes. These are mostly family recipes and provide a splendid standby for guests of any age — and with a few of these stocking up your cake tins you can afford to be generous.

 # Molly's Mother's Fruit Cake

Preparation time: 30 minutes
Cooking time: 1 hour 30 — 1 hour 40 minutes

Imperial (Metric)	American
12 oz (350 g) mixed fruit	*3 cups dried fruit*
4 oz (110 g) caster sugar	*1/2 cup caster sugar*
4 oz (110 g) margarine	*1/2 cup margarine*
8 oz (225 g) self-raising flour	*2 cups self-rising flour*
1 egg, beaten	*1 egg, beaten*
1/4 pint (275 ml) water	*just over 1/2 cup water*

1. Put margarine, water, fruit and sugar in pan. Bring slowly to boil, turn down heat and simmer for 20 minutes.
2. Allow to cool then add beaten egg and stir in flour.
3. Press into well greased 7 in (18 cm) cake tin or 2 lb bread tin and bake for 1½ hours at 300°F/150°C/Gas Mark 2. Test with a skewer and if not quite done leave for a further 10 minutes. Cool in tin.

Variations
1. Nut Cake — For dried fruit substitute 12 oz (230 g) (1½ cups) chopped mixed nuts.
2. Fruit and Nut Cake — For dried fruit substitute 6 oz (175 g) (1½ cups) raisins, 2 oz (50 g) (4 tablespoons) chopped peel, 2 oz (50 g) (4 tablespoons) chopped nuts.
3. Walnut and Cherry Cake — For dried fruit substitute 6 oz (175 g) (1½ cups) each of walnuts and glacé cherries.

 # Grandma's Chocolate Sponge

Preparation time: 20 minutes
Cooking time: 25 minutes

Imperial (Metric)

4 oz (110 g) butter
4 oz (110 g) caster sugar
4 oz (110 g) self-raising flour
2 eggs
2 tablespoons warm water
3 level tablespoons cocoa

American

½ cup butter
½ cup caster sugar
1 cup self-rising flour
2 eggs
2 tablespoons warm water
3 level tablespoons cocoa

1. Grease and line two 7 in (18 cm) sandwich tins. Cream butter and sugar. Beat in eggs.
2. Mix cocoa with flour and fold into mixture. Beat in 2 tablespoons warm water.
3. Divide mixture between the two tins and bake at 375°F/190°C/Gas Mark 5 for 25 minutes. Turn out on rack to cool and sandwich with cream or butter icing filling (see p. 143).

Variation

Mocha — reduce cocoa to 1½ level tablespoons and add 1 tablespoon of very strong black coffee.

 # Orange Tea Bread

Preparation time: 20 minutes
Cooking time: 1¼ hours

This is delicious just on its own but can also be sliced and buttered for tea.

Imperial (Metric)

10 oz (275 g) self-raising flour
4 oz (110 g) soft brown sugar
4 oz (110 g) soft margarine
1 egg, beaten
1 dessertspoon honey
juice and grated rind of 2 oranges

American

2½ cups self-rising flour
½ cup soft brown sugar
½ cup soft margarine
1 egg, beaten
1 dessertspoon honey
juice and grated rind of 2 oranges

1. Melt sugar, honey and margarine in a pan over very gentle heat. Allow to cool and add orange juice and rind and beaten egg.
2. Put all dry ingredients in a bowl and add orange mixture. Beat well.
3. Pour into large 2 lb (900 g) tin and bake at 325°F/170°C/Gas Mark 3 for about 1¼ hours. Leave in tin for ten minutes before turning out to cool on wire grid.

NB: If you use two separate 1 lb (450 g) tins the cooking time will be reduced to one hour.

Old-fashioned Gingerbread

Preparation time: 20 minutes
Cooking time: 1 hour

You probably already have your own gingerbread recipe — most families seem to have one — but if not, this one is a good traditional cake with plenty of flavour. And it keeps well too.

Imperial (Metric)	**American**
4 oz (110 g) plain flour	*1 cup all purpose flour*
2 oz (50 g) margarine	*¼ cup margarine*
3 oz (75 g) black treacle	*3 level tablespoons molasses*
1 oz (25 g) golden syrup	*1 level tablespoon maple syrup*
4 tablespoons milk	*4 tablespoons milk*
1 large egg, beaten	*1 large egg, beaten*
2 level teaspoons ground ginger	*2 level teaspoons ground ginger*
1 level teaspoon mixed spice	*1 level teaspoon mixed spice*
½ level teaspoon bicarbonate of soda	*½ level teaspoon bicarbonate of soda*
1 oz (25 g) caster sugar	*1 level tablespoon caster sugar*

1. Put treacle (molasses), syrup and margarine in pan over low heat until melted. Remove from heat and add milk and beaten egg.
2. Mix sifted flour, spices and bicarbonate of soda together in a bowl, then add the sugar and finally stir in the melted syrup mixture. Mix together well.
3. Grease and line the bottom of a 1 lb (450 g) loaf tin with greaseproof paper and scrape the cake mixture carefully into it, smoothing the top.
4. Bake in the centre of a cool oven at 300°F/150°C/Gas Mark 2 for an hour. Test with a skewer and if necessary leave another ten minutes.

Leave the gingerbread in the tin for at least one hour before turning out onto a wire grid to cool completely. This keeps very well and shouldn't be eaten until at least two days after baking.

Flat Currant Cake and Nut Crunch were Molly's father's favourite cakes and her mother made them every week of their married life. He enjoyed trying other cakes but those were the two he never tired of. They are both so easy to make that we often have them ourselves.

Flat Currant Cake

This is simply left over shortcrust pastry rolled out to about ¼ in (5 mm) thickness, sprinkled with currants, folded over and rolled lightly again. Place on a greased baking sheet in the bottom of the oven when you are baking other things, or when you have a casserole in the oven. It's ready when it turns slightly golden. Serve hot or cold cut in pieces with butter on top.

 # Nut Crunch

Preparation time: 10 minutes
Cooking time: 35 minutes

This recipe contains no nuts − the name refers to the texture. It's a sort of flapjack, always made in a square tin and cut into pieces about the size of a small chocolate bar.

Imperial (Metric)	**American**
4 oz (110 g) margarine	*½ cup margarine*
2 oz (50 g) dark brown sugar	*2 level tablespoons dark brown sugar*
2 tablespoons golden syrup	*2 tablespoons maple syrup*
4 oz (110 g) rolled oats	*1 cup rolled oats*

1. Melt sugar, margarine and syrup gently in a pan. Mix with the oats and press into a shallow 7 in (18 cm) square tin.
2. Bake for 35 minutes at 325°F/170°C/Gas Mark 3. Leave in tin to cool completely before turning out.

You'll also find the cake and biscuit recipes useful when entertaining one or two adults to a coffee morning or afternoon tea and here it's more enjoyable for both you and your guests if you make it a special occasion − even if they are regular visitors. Use your best embroidered cloth, your linen napkins and bone china cups. Set the table in the window or in a sheltered part of the garden on a fine day and take particular care with a few thinly cut sandwiches and offer a good selection of cake and biscuits or perhaps your own scones and home-made jam. Even old friends like to be made a fuss of and a beautifully set table makes anyone feel welcome. Make a point of wrapping up a few biscuits or a piece of cake they particularly enjoyed and be generous with your recipes. You will usually receive a few in return.

Dinner Parties

Giving dinner parties − or lunch parties − once you have retired is easier in many respects than for people in full time employment. For one thing, as I've already pointed out, the choice of guests is yours and with more time to plan it should be easier to avoid inviting guests whose personalities or diets put them on a collision course. Another advantage is that you have more time to look for inexpensive treats; one friend of ours recently regaled us with huge quantities of fresh asparagus, having discovered a — sadly temporary — cheap source of supply.

Having more time to plan means that you can make better use of your freezer if you have one, and you can spend more time on presentation. Flower arrangements in the dining room — small and low on the table and something more spectacular on a side table — make a lot of difference to the atmosphere of a meal. If we have only a few flowers in the garden we make a lot of use of greenery and berries and also mix in dried flowers and colourful leaves such as beech. An attractive dried flower arrangement, with the addition of one or two fresh flowers strategically placed with their stems either in small flasks of water or damp cotton wool, can look quite dramatic. Other time consuming touches like starched table linen, gleaming silver and glasses, butter curls, home-made cheese straws or a basket of melba toast make a tremendous difference.

Serve home-made pâté backed up with a little bought-in charcuterie and cheese — some supermarkets now sell selections of cheeses which are good value and save waste.

Try for an unusual display of vegetables — they can look stunning if arranged together on a large platter or perhaps as a wheel of, say, puréed carrot in the centre of broccoli 'spokes'. If you use fresh vegetables and fruit wherever possible, they alone make a dinner party into a feast.

Lots of fresh bread rolls — hot and home-made if possible — in different shapes add a generous touch and make the more expensive items go further.

One main course, as we've pointed out, is really all that's needed, with perhaps a soup in cold weather, but use the additional time you now have at your disposal to think up small easily prepared extras like *amuse-gueules* — such as sesame chick peas, crudités, curry biscuits or cheese straws, or bite-size vol au vents with a savoury filling — to serve with the aperitifs; and some home-made special sweets to accompany the coffee.

Remember, that unless you are entertaining someone with special dietary observations — in which case presumably you like them enough to make a few concessions — you are inviting people to share your meal and to eat and drink what you yourself enjoy.

This first dinner party menu was one we worked out for six people — that seems to be about the limit if the guests are not to divide into two groups. We made the pancakes a few days before and kept them in the freezer, but they would also be fine if you made them one day before and placed them well wrapped in a refrigerator or very cool place. We also made the frozen oranges several days before the dinner — mainly because they are rather time consuming.

Dinner Party Menu 1
Seafood Pancakes

Lemon Chicken
Assortment of Fresh Vegetables

Frozen Oranges

Seafood Pancakes

Preparation time: 30 minutes

Cooking time: 10 minutes

Wrap ready prepared pancakes − two per person − in foil, and place in bottom of a low oven to warm while you prepare filling.

Imperial (Metric)

4 oz (110 g) white fish (boneless)
4 oz (110 g) cooked crab or tuna
4 oz (110 g) cooked prawns (shelled)
2 oz (50 g) soft breadcrmbs
2 oz (110 g) butter
1 tablespoon chopped chives
1 large mushroom
¼ pint (150 ml) milk

American

4 oz white fish (boneless)
4 oz cooked crab or tuna
4 oz cooked prawns (shelled)
2 heaped tablespoons soft breadcrumbs
¼ cup butter
1 tablespoon chopped chives
1 large mushroon
just over ½ cup milk

1. Poach white fish and chopped mushroom in milk for five minutes; add other fish for further five minutes.
2. Drain. Melt butter and add to fish and all other ingredients. Mix together thoroughly. Season to taste.
3. Fill pancakes, evenly dividing mixture. Fold over and place in heatproof dish. Dot with flakes of butter and keep hot in bottom of oven.

Serve with either parsley butter or parsley sauce.

Lemon Chicken

Preparation time: 20 minutes

Cooking time: 1 hour 20 minutes − 1 hour 40 minutes

Imperial (Metric)

4 lb (1.8 kg) chicken
juice and grated rind of 2 lemons
2 oz (50 g) butter
1 tablespoon chopped parsley
1 tablespoon chopped lemon balm
(if possible)
2 oz (50 g) soft breadcrumbs
1 small grated onion

American

4 lb chicken
juice and grated rind of 2 lemons
¼ cup butter
1 tablespoon chopped parsley
1 tablespoon chopped lemon balm
(if possible)
2 heaped tablespoons soft breadcrumbs
1 small grated onion

1. Mix together all ingredients to make stuffing. Melt butter if it is firm and add a few more breadcrumbs if necessary to get a good 'bind'.
2. Stuff the body cavity as well as the breast of the chicken to enable the lemony flavour to permeate the whole bird, packing it in as far as you can. Secure flap with a skewer if necessary.
3. Smear the bird with butter, rub the squeezed lemons over it, season with salt

and pepper and put, breast up, in a large roasting tin with buttered paper on top. Cook at 375°F/190°C/Gas Mark 5 for 20 minutes per pound weight. Remove paper before last 20 minutes to brown the top nicely and check if the chicken needs an extra 20 minutes. Baste a couple of times during the cooking. If you are not sure it is cooked enough test with a skewer in the leg joint − the juice should be clear not pink.

Serve with a selection of fresh vegetables such as sautéed small potatoes, carrot purée, broccoli spears etc. Arrange them attractively.

Sauce
If a sauce is required, add 2 tablespoons lemon juice to the roasting tin juices, plus a little water, and bring to the boil. Blend 1 teaspoon cornflour (cornstarch) with a little water, stir into juices, sprinkle with parsley and serve.

 Frozen Oranges

Preparation time: 45 minutes
Cooking time: 8 minutes plus freezing time

These always excite comment when brought to the table. You can also follow the same recipe with large lemons.

Imperial (Metric)	American
6 medium oranges	*6 medium oranges*
2 small sweet oranges	*2 small sweet oranges*
4 eggs	*4 eggs*
6 oz (175 g) caster sugar	*¾ cup caster sugar*
6 oz (175 ml) double cream	*1 cup heavy cream*
2 tablespoons brandy	*2 tablespoons brandy*

1. Cut off small slice from top of each medium orange and very carefully scrape out all flesh and juice with a pointed spoon, taking care not to tear the rind.
2. Wind greaseproof paper around each orange shell and place them in the freezer for at least two hours.
3. Sieve flesh and press out juice. Finely grate rind of 1 sweet orange and place on one side. Remove peel from other sweet orange, scrape away pith and with scissors cut rind into very thin matchsticks about 4 in (10 cm) long. Put on one side. Add juice of 2 sweet oranges to other juice. Place this in pan with sugar, bring to boil and boil hard for five minutes.
4. Whisk up eggs, remove pan from heat and pour syrup onto eggs, whisking all the time. Allow to cool. Add finely grated rind and brandy. Whip up cream until thick then stir into orange mixture.
5. Remove frozen shells from freezer, carefully fill with ice cream, rounding the tops and place carefully in a large shallow dish, wedging paper between the oranges so that they won't tip over. Freeze overnight at least.

Garnish
In a heavy bottomed pan place 2 tablespoons sugar and 1 tablespoon water, bring

to boil and boil until syrupy. Add thin matchsticks of orange rind and cook until becoming transparent. Remove carefully with slotted spoon and drain on wire grid over absorbent paper. As they cool they will become brittle and can either be broken up to decorate tops of orange ices, or piled on top in long strands. Remove oranges from freezer five minutes before required as this is a soft ice cream.

Dinner Party Menu 2

Baked Eggs in Courgettes

Nini's Surprise Fish Pie

Zabaglione

Baked Eggs in Courgettes

Preparation time: 10 minutes
Cooking time: 12 minutes

Imperial (Metric)	**American**
12 small courgettes	*12 small zucchini*
4 oz (110 g) butter	*½ cup butter*
6 eggs	*6 eggs*
1 tablespoon parmesan cheese	*1 tablespoon parmesan cheese*
salt and pepper	*salt and pepper*

1. Slice courgettes and boil in water for two minutes. Drain and put on one side.
2. Butter six small ovenproof dishes and fill them with courgette slices, leaving a hollow in the centre. Melt the butter and pour over them.
3. Carefully break an egg into each nest. Add salt and pepper and sprinkle with parmesan. Put in preheated oven 400°F/200°C/Gas Mark 6, 12 minutes before required.

Serve with fresh rolls and butter or garlic bread, and encourage your guests to mop up the juices from the bottom of the dishes.

Nini's Surprise Fish Pie

Preparation time: 25 minutes
Cooking time: 30 minutes

I have never been very fond of tuna fish but ate this pie with great enjoyment before Nini told me what was in it. It looks and tastes splendid but you can of course use a can of salmon if you prefer.

Imperial (Metric)	American
13 oz (375 g) frozen puff pastry	*13 oz packet frozen puff pastry*
1½ oz (40 g) butter	*3 level tablespoons butter*
1½ oz (40 g) plain flour	*3 level tablespoons all purpose flour*
¾ pint (425 ml) milk	*just under 2 cups milk*
2 hard boiled eggs, chopped	*2 hardboiled eggs, chopped*
7 oz can (200 g) can tuna	*7 oz can tuna*
grated rind of a lemon	*grated rind of a lemon*
salt and pepper	*salt and pepper*

1. Melt butter, stir in flour, mix well and cook gently for two minutes. Remove from heat and gradually add milk. Return to heat and bring to boil, stirring until it thickens. Remove from heat.

2. Add chopped eggs, flaked tuna and lemon rind. Mix well together, season with salt and pepper.

3. Roll out pastry and cut into two 8 in x 4 in (20 x 10 cm) pieces. Place one on baking sheet, cover with filling leaving a gap round the edges. Damp edges, cover with other pastry, press edges together, flute along the sides, cut three slits in top of pastry with small sharp knife and brush with a little milk or beaten egg. Bake in centre of oven for 25 minutes at 425°F/220°C/Gas Mark 7.

Serve with a selection of fresh vegetables or a green salad.

 Zabaglione

Preparation time: 5 minutes

Cooking time: 2 minutes

This is always a success and although it has to be made at the last minute this isn't a problem if you have all the ingredients ready.

Imperial (Metric)	American
6 egg yolks	*6 egg yolks*
6 tablespoons sherry	*6 tablespoons sherry*
3 oz (75 g) caster sugar	*3 tablespoons caster sugar*
sponge fingers	*sponge fingers*

Beat egg yolks and sugar until foaming. Put into top of a double saucepan or a basin over hot water and stir as you slowly pour in sherry. Whisk up vigorously for a minute, transfer to warm glasses and serve with sponge fingers or Langues de Chat.

If you prefer a meat dish instead of fish for the main course, you could try an old fashioned steak and kidney pie which never fails to please guests with hearty appetites.

 # Steak and Kidney Pie

Preparation time: about 1 hour
Cooking time: 3 hours

Imperial (Metric)	American
8 oz (225 g) flaky pastry	8 oz flaky pastry
1½ lb (700 g) stewing steak	1½ lb stewing steak
8 oz (225 g) kidney	8 oz kidney
1 onion	1 onion
tablespoon vegetable fat	tablespoon vegetable fat
salt and pepper	salt and pepper
1 pint (570 ml) stock	2½ cups stock
flour	flour

1. Trim any fat from steak and kidney and cut into small cubes. Roll in a little flour and brown meat quickly in hot fat. Remove to a large saucepan. Add stock, sliced onion and seasoning. Bring to boil then simmer with lid on for about 1½ hours until meat is nearly cooked.

2. Roll out pastry on floured board a little larger than 1½ in deep pie dish. Up-turn pie dish and cut out pastry to cover to size. With sharp knife cut a pastry trimming for edge of pie dish and press into greased rim. Spoon meat and onion into dish, add gravy except for about ¼ pint (150 ml) (½ cup), moisten pastry rim, cover with pastry top and press down edges. Flute with a knife. Make a hole in centre of pie and decorate with pastry leaves.

3. Bake at 425°F/220°C/Gas Mark 7 for 30 minutes, then lower heat to 350°F/180°C/Gas Mark 4 for another 45 to 60 minutes until golden brown. Serve extra gravy in a jug.

Menu 3

Pâtés de Maison
Sesame Crackers, Cheese Straws

Pork and Apple Kebabs

Ginger Cream Log

Select any of the pâtés, such as smoked salmon or mushroom. Serve perhaps two and a plate of home-made rolls and sesame crackers. This is also a good time to produce your cheese straws.

 # Pork and Apple Kebabs

Preparation time: 20 minutes
Cooking time: 20 minutes

Imperial (Metric)	**American**
1 lb (450 g) pork fillet	*1 lb pork fillet*
6 prunes	*6 prunes*
lemon juice	*lemon juice*
apples (2 or 3)	*apples (2 or 3)*
24 button mushrooms	*24 button mushrooms*
salt and pepper	*salt and pepper*

1. Cut the pork fillet into neat cubes, peel and core apples, cut into cubes and drop them into lemon juice until required.
2. Thread ingredients onto skewers − if the skewers are very long add a few cubes of bread − brush them with oil and grill (broil) under a medium heat for about 20 minutes. Turn them several times. Season with salt and pepper.
3. Serve on a warm dish with fresh sage leaves if possible − the heat will release their fragrance − or parsley will do. Creamy mashed potatoes and a green vegetable go well with this dish.

The Ginger Cream Log (see p. 95) somehow always seems perfect after a pork dish and can of course be made beforehand.

Drinks

It's your party, so whether it's a cheese and wine buffet or a formal dinner party the extent of the choice you offer your guests need not be greater than their accepting what is on offer or going without. With a buffet, for example, offer a choice of white or red wine or simply opt for a rosé which is even simpler and, like champagne, goes with practically everything.

Champagne may go with everything but it's a rich man's cop out − besides which, if you are going to do it properly you need a different type of champagne to accompany different courses and that can be very expensive.

One glass of champagne, on the other hand, served as an aperitif, can turn a dinner into an occasion and one bottle should be enough for six people. For lesser occasions a bottle of Sekt − which is the German equivalent − or any sparkling wine made by the methode champenoise (domestic) is more than adequate and usually works out at less than a third of the price of even the cheapest champagne.

Alternatively a 'poor man's champagne' of ice cold tonic water with a dash of dry sherry works out even cheaper. Pour in the kitchen, serve in champagne flutes, and don't give the secret away unless asked!

Bottle parties can work well provided all the guests are relieved of their offerings at the door. When we were doing a spell of lotus eating on the Riviera we found that the best thing was to soak sliced oranges in the cheapest brandy with sugar and a couple of bottles of red wine. Leave in a large container overnight and then add the guests' offerings as they arrive − always leaving a couple of drops in the bottom of the more expensive bottles for a rainy day. Use fizzy lemonade to make the mixture spin out and exercise the host's prerogative of frequent tasting to avoid over-dilution.

Home-made Wine

Home-made wine can be splendid and is a real money saver; but it should be enjoyed only by consenting adults in private. In other words — unless you are a very experienced and successful wine maker — keep it for yourself and the· immediate family.

We find we can make a more than acceptable table wine for everyday drinking by buying cans of grape juice — red is easiest to start with — and following the directions on the can. All you need is a gallon jar with an airlock device, a couple of empty sweet jars, a few wine bottles and a length of plastic tubing — and you're in business. Once you have made wine successfully from grape juice you may like to try other types of home-made wine from your own fruits or stuff gathered from the country. There are several good books on the subject in local libraries and bookshops.

Later on you could join a Wine Making Circle which should yield a lot of help and advice, besides enabling you to get to know people to whom you can offer your own wine when you invite them for drinks.

Buying Wines and Other Drinks

When buying spirits for cooking, it's often cheaper to take along a small bottle to your local pub and ask for a couple of measures. In the same way if, say, you want to offer guests a Pernod before the meal and a brandy afterwards, you don't have to buy full bottles.

Use some of your retirement leisure to seek out unusual drinks which need not be expensive — like Kir, for instance. This was invented by Bishop Kir of Dijon who became fed up with being offered champagne made by a rival region at every dinner party banquet. The drink consists of white wine with Creme de Cassis and as you do not need an expensive white wine and have probably made your own blackcurrant syrup from fruit bushes in your garden, it can be a very reasonable way of giving your friends something unusual.

By and large, in wine as in most things you get what you pay for, and if you need a fine wine for an extra-special occasion most good wine merchants will be glad to advise you. Should you wish to learn more about wine there is a wine appreciation society in most towns which your wine merchant will be able to tell you about and he himself may hold regular wine tastings.

In Britain there is great competition in the wine trade at the moment, especially between the large wine store chains and the supermarkets, which means that there are bargains to be had. Look for chains which employ a Master of Wine to select their wines and one who is prepared to put his name to his choices — the combination of his expertise and the chain's buying power can often lead to real bargains, especially in the lower ranges.

Another thing to look for is a wine which comes from the borders of a well known — and therefore expensive — wine growing area. Avoid anonymous bottles and, if you can, wine which has travelled from its point of origin in container trucks. Look instead for estate bottled wine or wine which has been bottled by wine shippers or co-operatives close to the vineyards.

Most wine will keep reasonably well after being opened, which means that even if you are by yourself you have no need either to go without wine with your meals or to drink the whole bottle at a sitting.

Wine is in fact the ideal accompaniment to 'cooking in retirement', whether you use it to cook with, drink it with the meal or merely sip it contemplatively while you decide what delicious dish to prepare next.

We hope that *Cooking in Retirement* will have been some help in making such decisions easier and the cooking itself more fun, as well as enabling you to keep fit, make friends and save money.

If it does all this and helps you to enjoy your retirement as it should be enjoyed, Molly and I will be well pleased.

Index